VIRTUAL CORPORATE UNIVERSITIES
A Matrix of Knowledge and Learning
for the New Digital Dawn

INTEGRATED SERIES IN INFORMATION SYSTEMS

Series Editors

Professor Ramesh Sharda
Oklahoma State University

Prof. Dr. Stefan Voß
Universität Hamburg

Other published titles in the series:

E-BUSINESS MANAGEMENT: *Integration of Web Technologies with Business Models*/ Michael J. Shaw

VIRTUAL CORPORATE UNIVERSITIES
*A Matrix of Knowledge and Learning
for the New Digital Dawn*

Walter R. J. Baets
*Nyenrode University
The Netherlands*

Gert Van der Linden
*donedeal
Monte Carlo, Monaco*

KLUWER ACADEMIC PUBLISHERS
Boston / Dordrecht / London

Distributors for North, Central and South America:
Kluwer Academic Publishers
101 Philip Drive
Assinippi Park
Norwell, Massachusetts 02061 USA
Telephone (781) 871-6600
Fax (781) 871-9045
E-Mail: kluwer@wkap.com

Distributors for all other countries:
Kluwer Academic Publishers Group
Post Office Box 322
3300 AH Dordrecht, THE NETHERLANDS
Telephone 31 786 576 000
Fax 31 786 576 254
E-mail: services@wkap.nl

 Electronic Services <http://www.wkap.nl>

Library of Congress Cataloging-in-Publication Data

A C.I.P. Catalogue record for this book is available from the Library of Congress.

Baets, W. & Van der Linden, G. / VIRTUAL CORPORATE UNIVERSITIES: *A Matrix of Knowledge and Learning for the New Digital Dawn*

ISBN 1-4020-7382-8

Printed on acid-free paper.

Printed in United Kingdom by Biddles/IBT Global

Contents

Contributors

WALTER BAETS holds the Philips Chair in Information and Communication Technology at Nyenrode University, the Netherlands Business School. He is director of Notion, the Nyenrode Institute for Knowledge Management and Virtual Education, a competence center sponsored by Achmea, Microsoft, Philips and Sara Lee/DE. Walter graduated in econometrics and operations research at the University of Antwerp (Belgium), did postgraduate studies in business administration at Warwick Business School (UK), and was awarded a Ph.D. from the University of Warwick in Industrial and Business Studies. After pursuing a career in business, he held positions in the academia in Belgium, Russia, the Netherlands and Spain.

Walter is active as a researcher, teacher, and consultant in the areas of knowledge management, virtual learning, emergent strategic behavior based on complexity theory, and the use of artificial intelligence and IT in organizations. With Gert Van der Linden, Walter Baets published *The Hybrid Business School: Developing Knowledge Management through Management Learning* (Prentice Hall, 2000). He is editor of *A Collection of Essays on Complexity and Management* (World Scientific, 1999), and acted as co-editor with Bob Galliers of *IT and Organizational Transformation* (Wiley, 1998). Walter also wrote *Organizational Learning and Knowledge Technologies in a Dynamic Environment* (Kluwer Academic Publishers, 1998).

Email: w.baets@nyenrode.nl

GERT VAN DER LINDEN has been involved in conceptualizing, designing, and coordinating several innovative management development programs and strategies as well as corporate MBA and leadership/ top executive programs for several major European, Japanese, and American companies.

A founding member of *donedeal*, a boutique firm focusing on launching businesses into their best configured competitive market space, and (re)launching underperforming and distressed companies whilst unearthing authentic potential, Gert acquired boardroom experience and previously acted as chief executive of Areopa - an intellectual capital and change management consulting organization active throughout Europe and Southeast Asia. Prior to that, he was Managing Director of Global Paradoxes – a cutting-edge strategy-based management consulting firm.

Gert Van der Linden has acted as an interim/ transition executive, advisor and consultant for several international companies, top executives and senior managers, advising them on reinventing and deploying innovative long-term visions, defining and implementing strategic change, business concepts, adaptive, growth, and turnaround processes, brand identities and brand strategies. Most of his 15 years of professional experience is in technology, telecom, e-commerce and other fast-moving sectors and companies, working for European, American, and Japanese companies across Europe and the US.

Gert was a visiting professor at several business schools and management institutes in France, Spain, Sweden, and the Netherlands. In addition, he has published more than 20 articles and cases in various journals. Gert is co-author of *The Hybrid Business School: Developing Knowledge Management through Management Learning* (2000 – Prentice Hall). Gert Van der Linden graduated in organizational psychology, and did postgraduate studies in management and technology at the Free University of Brussels. He holds a Ph.D. in Business Administration from the University of Groningen (The Netherlands).

Email: vdlinden@donedeal.mc

Preface

Over the past years, business schools have been experimenting with distance learning and online education. In many cases, this new technology has not brought the anticipated results. Questions raised by online education can be linked to the fundamental problem of education and teaching, and more specifically to the models and philosophy of education and teaching. This book offers a source for new thoughts about those processes in view of the use of new technologies. We consider learning as a key-strategic tool for new strategies, innovation, and significantly improving organizational effectiveness. The book blends the elements of knowledge management, and (organizational as well as individual) learning. As such, we envision learning, and the combination of learning, its application and sharing, and the creation of new knowledge. It is, however, not just a case of "more" technology, but a fusion of a novel dynamic learner (student) -driven learning concept, the management and creation of dynamic knowledge, and next-generation technologies to generic business, organizational and managerial processes, and the development of human capital. Obviously, the implications of online learning go far beyond the field of business as presented in this book.

Companies aim at leveraging learning with knowledge management in a process that reinforces both. Management clearly has some ideas about the driving wheel of this process, and business schools should be able to incorporate those ideas into its programs. In order to realize this, however, both parties must have a common understanding of their philosophy and purpose of education and knowledge management. We are still far away from that common understanding and this book attempts to bring these two worlds together.

This book addresses the interests of both companies and business schools in trying to leverage the joint purpose of virtual life-long learning with knowledge management. It goes far beyond advocating this purpose, but explains the value behind it, discusses the theories developed around it, and gives clear guidelines for development, both for companies and business schools alike.

Companies want to learn from their experiences and want to share those lessons amongst employees. Employees should learn from past experiences and benefit from best practices that get translated into best principles. Best practices are interesting stories. Best principles are lessons learned that can be applied in new projects. If the reader is interested in setting up a platform for knowledge sharing and/or collaborative learning, this book will definitely be of help. It combines the principles learned about the pedagogical processes and approaches with the expectations of companies to deliver just in time, just appropriate, just enough, i.e., J-learning.

This book also shares innovative ideas and gives practical guidelines for those companies and educational institutions that want to learn from the experience of web-based teaching. We need to walk the path of learning from experience as we can only offer material for reflection and self-learning. The reader is guided through this process and eventually given a concrete blueprint to define the appropriate learning and knowledge management. We offer a complete business case for developing a learning and knowledge environment with the appropriate technological solutions.

Join us on an exploratory tour of these exiting forms of management development where you can expect to reap an understanding of the following issues.

Chapter 1 discusses the present economic environment, such as the new economic realities, the drivers of change that companies encounter these days, and their impact on organizations. It is the general collapse of time and space that has lead to the creation of the knowledge era, where we now operate, with its particularities. The impact of the technological evolution gets particular attention since it is often the cause of disruptive innovation and discontinuities in corporate development. The appropriate use of Information Communication Technology (ICT) remains an important concern of corporations today.

We come to an understanding of some of the fundamental concepts of the knowledge era by relating it to the dynamic behavior of systems. This allows the reader to consider knowledge and learning from a completely different paradigm, namely the paradigm of learning by doing and learning from experience.

Chapter 2 describes the impact of the knowledge economies on the corporate environment, where changing managerial roles and the necessary managerial competencies are identified. We witness a movement from classical control-based management to a more networked organization. As managers have more hybrid roles, operating on different levels in different functions and as they become more "part of the scene and the play itself" rather than just the director, we pinpoint the competencies needed in order to fulfil this new hybrid role.

Another important development in the corporate environment is the role that information increasingly plays, and more particularly the dynamic process by which information is continually created and adapted. This dynamic property of information contrasts strongly with the static character of Information Systems (IS) development, which tends to be fatally out of date by the time it is finished. A promising area is therefore the one of adaptive and learning applications - applications that learn and change 'by doing.' Some attention is given to artificial neural networks as a practical approach of a learning software development tool.

The relationships between knowledge and experience, learning and mental models, knowledge and learning are discussed, in order to clarify what one wants to create by knowledge management available via a learning platform. Also, the complex process of learning and the concept of organizational learning is brought into the context of the (post)modern company. The book intentionally focuses on concepts to support the framework, and delivers practical guidelines to people who want to incorporate our ideas and programs into their own companies and business institutes.

Chapter 3 focuses on the business education environment. Some of the criticisms from business on business schools and business education are investigated. An inventory of the experiences of management development is made in its broad sense and the book deals with phenomena such as open learning, corporate universities and corporate MBAs. Eventually this leads to the development of an educational competency approach, with detail concerning the program design and the teaching philosophy.

Building a virtual corporate learning platform, of course, necessitates some state of the art information technology. Chapter 4 shows the leverage between knowledge management and virtual education, based on the potential of information and knowledge technologies such as case-based reasoning systems, group decision support systems, artificial neural networks, and knowledge platforms. Insight about what learning environments can offer and the latest developments in communication technology draw the overall picture of the combination between knowledge management and virtual education - what we call the Hybrid Business School.

Chapter 5 entails a detailed discussion of the concept of the Hybrid Business School. We pay attention to the necessary building blocks, but equally describe their underlying process and concrete realizations. This chapter emphasizes what happens today in online lifelong learning, focusing on the concerns of companies and practising managers. Virtual learning melts together with knowledge management to create a self-learning and ever-adaptive knowledge platform for companies.

Chapter 6 portrays illustrations and examples of the Hybrid Business School concept. It offers three concrete cases, an example of a corporate learning project as well as two illustrations of degree programs that make clear that how the concept is constructed and how its particular philosophy can be realized.

Chapter 7 presents a detailed blueprint for implementation, both for companies and business institutes, which can be used as a methodology that supports and accompanies the reader on his journey of creating his own Hybrid Business School together with the appropriate learning and knowledge management environment based on specific situations, learning needs, and learning cultures. Supported by the intelligent use of technologies, the ICT platforms dynamically create individualized learning solutions for companies and institutions that allow people to learn, experiment, and develop. The development never stops, but is now done by the only one that really knows his/her needs: the learner him/ herself.

We have included a special chapter in appendix that surveys previous research in this area, and identifies research questions. These questions cover learning goals, pedagogical approaches, learning models, assessment of effectiveness of the new virtual learning technologies, and technical as well as process issues and challenges. We document possible approaches that can be taken to answer some of them. Readers with a scientific interest will appreciate the details about the origins of most theories in the book and about how they are related to reality and current research projects. A wealth of references are included to allow readers to enter the scientific literature on this topic.

Gert Van der Linden

Walter Baets

Acknowledgements

In these decentralized times, we owe thanks to a variety of people.

At one end, we are grateful to Rob Baak for his technical advice, "Mr." Maddox for the inspiring title, and Richard Walker for carrying out research related to the appendix chapter.

At one other end, we thank Gary Folven of Kluwer, Stefan Voss at the Technische Universität of Braunschweig, and Ramesh Sharda at Oklahoma State University for their constructive comments and reviews that helped us to reshape the book.

In between, we thank all those we have disturbed, interrupted, discussed, argued, and corresponded with us during our years of research and reflection. We also thank those who nurtured, cultivated, and enriched us … and still do.

They all know who they are.

Chapter 1

Economic Environment and Drivers of Change

1.   NEW ECONOMIC REALITIES

The workplace, the company, and the world are not even remotely what they were ten years ago. There has never been a time in history when changes have evolved so rapidly, discontinuously, and nonlinearly while affecting so many aspects of everyday and corporate life. Sure, changes are not novel to history, yet the quantitative and qualitative leaps (flux), and the increasing complexity has never been experienced in such a way. As a result, corporate life has become and is becoming more complex, complicated, and paradoxical.

Several economic trends in the world are directly related to the challenges faced within companies today. Trade blocks and free trade zones, deregulation and privatization, a shaky world economy, the opening of emergent countries and markets, the EMU and the introduction of the EURO, and the technological interconnectedness of the world, characterize the expansion of the economic environment yet make it a much "smaller" marketplace than it used to be.

Deregulation increasingly has an impact on competition worldwide. As depicted by the telecommunications industry in South America or the airline industry in Europe, however, it is a complicated process. The privatization of companies such as British Airways or France Telecom describes the difficult process of the shift in "corporate" focus and cultural change, i.e. the

1

impact of competition, disappearance of state protectionism, and governments slowly backing out of the marketplace where they had previously guarded their own interests so heavily. Both opportunities and competition are increasing with the removal of the (quasi) monopolies from many countries. At the same time, there is the emergence of trade blocs in every region of the world, as regions push to safeguard their own interests and protect their own industries from the increasing competition and deregulation which can now reach all corners of the globe. In other words, we are witnessing a shift from protectionism within a given country to protectionism within a given region, allowing for much greater competition and movement of goods and services.

As global borders disappear and markets reach much further, opportunities grow, and the number of competitors and complexity increase. In how many cases do we really see global competition as opposed to multi-domestic or crossnational competition? Few products are really global products: not McDonalds' hamburger, not Boeing's 737, not Ford's Focus. Each of these products is tailored to local preferences or specifics. Besides, with the advent of technology, distance is no longer a major disincentive to trade as it is not always necessary to be present in a market physically to do business in it. Technology also enables "unconventional" competitors to enter business. A single person or a new company or competitor can become a new player due to the low cost of technology. Think about the myriad small firms specialized in web design. In 1980 4.5 MIPS (millions of instructions per second) cost about $4.5 million. By 1990, 4.5 MIPS cost about $100,000. It was projected that by the year 2000, and indeed already, this same amount of computer power will cost only $10,000. In terms of human resources, that would have equaled 210 people in 1980, and just 0.125 of a person today. The single person in a backroom might be the extreme example, but never before have so many people worked in small companies.

Since the mid-nineties we have witnessed another wave of mergers and acquisitions (M&As), joint ventures, alliances and partnerships. Some 32,000 alliances have been formed around the world in the past three years (1995-1998), three-quarters of them across borders. Alliances now account for 18% of revenues of America's companies. Particularly in the pharmaceutical, automotive, airline, and financial services industries, companies see it as a strategy to grow. They come in many shapes and sizes: as joint ventures, minority stakes, co-branding, marketing alliances, co-manufacturing projects, R&D agreements, and so on.

There was also rampant activity in M&As in the 1980s, but with a very different strategy. In the eighties, the goal was diversification, whereas recently, the strategy has been to focus on the core business and core competencies, and to look for compatible partners who either add to marketshare (consolidation), have a strong presence in a particular geographical area or a particular market segment, offer compatibility in the value chain, or add the services on which the firm no longer wants to focus. Core competencies bundle strategic resources and core technologies, supported by capabilities, and are harmonized in a governing process. Metaphorically pictured as a tree, the root system is core competence, the trunk is core business, the major limbs are core products, and the leaves, flowers, and fruits are end products.

It is economies of skill that in the first instance underlies this trend. A good example of these economies can be seen in a June 1998 joint venture in which Psion, Nokia, Ericsson, and Motorola, came together to form a new company called Symbian. Symbian licenses, develops and supports the EPOC operating system - a robust, reliable realtime operating system. EPOC is optimized for smartphones and communicators, allowing licensees to design their own user interfaces and select and add relevant applications. This will allow the development of a wide range of compatible devices with different designs and functionality. It is a very good example of an entity formed among several competitors in the product space, working together in the technology space. Each contributes its own core competencies, and as a whole, the company becomes a powerful entity pushing innovation.

Finally, there is a great increase in socio-political complexities, which directly affect the marketplace and the way business is conducted. The Asian recession and its consequences reach every corner of the globe, and also has a grave impact on western economies. The introduction of the EURO, African and Russian instabilities, turmoil in the Middle East, ethnic conflicts in Eastern Europe, the consequences of natural disasters in Central America, and the changing European political environment all contribute to an increased uncertainty.

These elements and others, the dynamics and accelerations between them drive new economic realities. This new economic age imposes a new competitive landscape, global in nature with increasing environmental turbulences and uncertainties. Underlying, and in some cases driving these economic trends is the technological revolution. Technology has changed the shape of the world, the shape of the marketplace, the shape of the company, and the shape of everyday life.

1.1. Technological Revolution

Technology enables us to work and live differently than we have in the past. Technology promotes flexibility in a working structure, allowing people to work from anywhere, not confined to a physical space. This creates more convenience and higher productivity of employees, leading to generally more efficiency, less stress, and a happier workforce.

Why call it a revolution? One of the most important attributes of the technological revolution is the importance of radical and dramatic innovations. These dramatic and radical innovations, and the high frequency with which they occur, have created the competitive accelerator - shorter and steeper business cycles - making speed a crucial factor in remaining competitive. In the late eighties and early nineties, US car manufacturers needed 5 to 7 years to develop and introduce a new model to the market place. Chrysler and the Neon illustrate how the US manufacturers understood the importance of development time. Recently, Nissan announced it has an 18-month cycle and Toyota holds the record of 15 months. In other industries, every "generation" of new products has to be based on a new technological generation in order to be competitive. Can you imagine now buying a computer with a 133Mhz processor that not that long ago seemed the high end of the market?

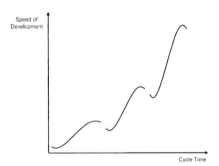

Figure 1-1. The discontinuity of technological developments

In other words, the technological edge increases considerably in a discontinuous way - it's not just a linear evolvement (movement) in time. If we envision a graph of the past business cycle, it ascends linearly at a slope of 45 degrees. The business cycle of today has steep vertical leaps along the graph and a higher slope due to the increasing technological developments that speed up the cycle. This means that products have a shorter life cycle, and as a result they must be brought to market much more quickly. Every aspect of the business, however, must work more efficiently as competition mounts on all sides. To progress at the same rate as the competition now means to be running faster and faster on a treadmill. It is important not to forget that running on the treadmill cannot mean companies can afford always to stay in the same place competitively. Like the American philosopher Rogers said, even if you are on the right track, you will be run over if you stand still. Speed is not only important, but imperative for those who want to be the leaders in their industry.

The time factor brings an important value-adding factor into a company as business value is added by pushing speed, a deceitfully, but seemingly simple, task. The average competitive advantage a company enjoys due to a particular strategic "edge" over its competition is about 24 to 28 months. If companies can push this limit and successfully bring products more quickly to market, they will reap the vast profits it produces. On the other hand, if nothing is done to sustain that competitive edge, then the 24-month period will be the extent of its glory in the marketplace. Companies must continuously invest in R&D and keep innovating while increasing their cycles in order to remain competitive. Firms must be continuously learning and developing their core competencies in a dynamic way. They must put emphasis on information and knowledge-building infrastructures. In other words, a focus on speed alone is not going to create added value. But on the other hand, if everything else is right in the company except speed, then the company will likely get run over and left in the dust.

This also illustrates how technology can modify value activities, transform linkages in the value chain, between value chains of other stakeholders and even enter the value chains of these stakeholders.

1.2. Collapse of Time

This compression of time has also been shown in the increase of modular manufacturing approaches and just-in-time systems. Volkswagen of Germany takes it even further by physically incorporating suppliers in its plants. Suppliers have their own manufacturing within Volkswagen's manufacturing plant in order to compress the notion of JIT even more. Just-in-time becomes real time. Portable computers and portable phones allow claims adjusters to make instant decisions, resulting in claims that are settled in minutes rather than weeks or months. Speed saves the insurance company money, it helps customer morale, improves accuracy, lowers prices, and sells. The "need for speed" illustrates how technology can modify value activities, transform linkages in the value chain, between value chains of other stakeholders and even enter the value chains of these stakeholders. Also, in many cases the compression of time drives the wave of alliances, joint ventures and partnerships. More time is put in reducing time, in shortened horizons. But at the same time, an increasing amount of executives feel the need to invest more time in the longer term view, in long-term horizons, as they understand that instant success takes ... time. And as time is a journey of perception, cultural and value-laden patterns have a high stake in this discussion.

1.3. Collapse of Space

As borders disappear, markets reach much further. In global competition, not only do the opportunities grow, but also the number of competitors and complexity increase. Much of this opportunity has been created by world economic development described earlier. With the advent of technology, distance is no longer a major disincentive to trade. As a result approximately 95 percent of U.S. business executives made globalization an important part of their firm's strategy. Implementation seems to be a more difficult issue. In how many cases do we really see a global approach as opposed to multidomestic or cross-national approach? In most cases, companies pursue separate strategies in each of its foreign markets while viewing the competitive challenge independently from market to market. And again, few products are really global products. From an organizational point of view, globalization never has been further away as companies have experienced myriad difficulties in working with their local subsidiaries. Clashes between local cultures and corporate cultures that offer equal standards of service, and dynamics and management between subsidiaries and corporate headquarters, increase distances rather than decrease them.

1.4. The knowledge era

An important and remarkable evolution in what we still call today the industrial world is that it is no longer industrial. We witness a rapid transition from an industrial society into a knowledge society. The knowledge society is based on the growing importance of knowledge as the so-called fourth production factor. Many products and certainly all services have a high research and development cost, whereas the production cost itself is rather low. Developing and launching a new operating system like

Windows costs a huge amount of investment for Microsoft, which makes the first copy very expensive, but any further copies have a very low production costs. Having a number of consultants working for a company is a large investment for a consulting company, so when they are actively working on a project, their marginal cost is close to zero. Having the knowledge base, which means having the consultants available is expensive. Their real work for a client is relatively cheaper. Even the best example of industrial production in the Western part of the world, car manufacturing, became increasingly knowledge-based. More than 40% of the sales price of a car is due to research, development and marketing.

We still talk about the industrialized countries, since most of our thinking is still based on concepts of industrial production dating back to the earlier parts of this century. What we have observed, though, is that increasingly companies get involved in optimizing supply chains and that those supply chains evolve into demand and supply chains. The following step consists of those chains supported with information technology (IT) in order to increase efficiency. The strange thing that happens in a next stage is that a progressive use of IT puts pressure on the existence itself of the chain. The better a chain is integrated based on IT, the more pressure gets created which makes the chain explode into a network. Particularly in such circumstances, the owner of the knowledge base manages the process. Network structures evolve around knowledge centers. Companies manage brands and outsource most of the chain itself. Extreme examples of this approach are Calvin Klein, Benetton and Nike. Again, knowledge, and particularly the capacity to manage, create and share knowledge is becoming the center of the successful company. This can be translated via brand management, direct marketing to targeted clients, etc., but it is the visual part of the evolution from an industrial market into a knowledge-based market. Knowledge becomes yet another attribute of the changing economic reality.

Knowledge in a company has different forms and most commonly one regroups these forms into three categories. Tacit knowledge is mainly based on experiences while explicit knowledge refers to the rules and procedures that a company follows. Cultural knowledge is the environment in which the company and the individual (within the company) operates.

Different forms of knowledge are crafted by various different activities. Conversion of knowledge takes place based on the tacit and explicit knowledge that a person possesses or has access to. The creation of knowledge very often takes place during joint work sessions, such as brainstorming and management meetings, etc. Equally important but more difficult to capture is knowledge processing via assimilation. Very often, assimilation is based on cultural knowledge as a first input, reinforced with tacit knowledge that often collapses with explicit rules and regulations. It seems important to stress, however, that knowledge management is only the 'sufficient' condition. The 'necessary' condition in order to deal with new economic realities is the boundary conditions for knowledge management and that is the learning culture of the company.

Above all, knowledge management and learning is an attitude and a way of working with management. It is an overall approach that goes beyond the addition of a number of functional tactics. One could even say that it is a kind of philosophy of management, rather than a science. This process is one of redefining the goal of the company from a profit making or share-value increasing entity to a knowledge-creating unit. The first type of organization has a rather short-term focus, whereas the latter type has a more visionary and long-term one.

The aim of the company is no longer purely growth as such, but rather it becomes sustainable development and renewal. Hence, organizations not only need knowledge, they also need the skills and competencies to dynamically update and put knowledge into practice. This results in the need for organizations to learn continuously and to continuously improve their actions through the acquired knowledge. Hence, organizations should embrace the philosophy of the learning organizations, the process being organizational learning.

A learning organization enables each of its members to continually learn and helps to generate new ideas and thinking. By this process, organizations continuously learn from their own and others, experiences, adapt and improve their efficiency towards the achievement of their goal. In a way, learning organizations aim to convert themselves into "knowledge-based" organizations by creating, acquiring and transferring knowledge so as to improve their planning and actions.

In order to build a learning organization, or a corporate learning culture, companies should be skilled at systematic problem-solving, learning from their own experience, learning from the experiences of others, processing knowledge quickly and efficiently through the organization and experimenting with new approaches. Developments in information and knowledge technologies make it increasingly possible to achieve these competitive needs and skills.

2.   COMPLEX DYNAMIC BEHAVIOR

In the previous section, we described the drivers of change within new economic realities. It becomes apparent that managerial complexity not only increases, but it also becomes different. On one hand, a higher degree of complexity in management as well as dissipating structures force companies into quantitative and qualitative leaps of improvement. On the other hand, due to a faster change and higher velocity in the world economy some appearances become clearer than they ever have been before. What we observe today while studying market behavior, is that we can no longer speak of an objective world where interactions can be described in linear terms, where words have singular meanings, and where prediction and control are paramount.

In the past, identifiable when market change moved slower, we got used to thinking in terms of reasonably linear behavior as markets and industries appeared to be more stable or mature. Concretely, one thought one could easily forecast future behavior based on past observations and in many respects we developed complex (and sometimes complicated) methods to extrapolate linear trends. But in reality, markets did not and do not behave in a linear way. The future is not a simple extrapolation of the past. A given action can lead to several possible outcomes ("futures"), some of which are disproportionate in size to the action itself. The "whole" is therefore not equal to the sum of the "parts." This contrasting perspective evolved from complexity and chaos theory. Complexity theory challenges the traditional management assumptions by embracing nonlinear and dynamic behavior of systems, and by noting that human activity allows for the possibility of emergent behavior. Emergence can be defined as the overall system behavior that stems from the interaction of many participants - behavior that cannot be predicted or even "envisioned" from the knowledge of what each component of a system does. Organizations, for example, often experience change processes as emergent behavior. Complexity theory also tells corporate executives that beyond a certain point, increased knowledge of complex, dynamic systems does little to improve the ability to extend the horizon of predictability for those systems. No matter how much one knows about the weather, no matter how powerful the computers, specific long-range predictions are not possible.

The focus on nonlinear behavior of markets collides with the traditional positivist and Cartesian view of the world. That positivist perspective translated in the traditional management literature - the stuff that most MBAs are taught - describes *the* world in terms of variables and matrices, and within a certain system of coordinates. Exact and objective numbers are needed in order to create models while simulations can offer a 'correct' picture of what to expect. Particularly business schools have welcomed this 'scientific' way of dealing with management problems as the one which could bring business schools up to the "scientific" level of the beta sciences. It is clear that much of the existing management practice, theory, and "remedies" based on the positivist view are limited by their dependence on several inappropriate assumptions as they don't reflect business and market behavior. Linear and static methods are the ones that are taught in business schools. Therefore, markets have to be linear and static. As we know they are not.

It seems important to elaborate a little more on positivist thinking as we want to propose later a challenging view on management and management education. In order to do that, we take a brief look into some positivist epistemology. Epistemology is concerned with understanding the origin, nature and validity of knowledge, i.e., the science or theory of (in our case) positivism. These fundamental assumptions built into the epistemological outlook plays a vital role in determining practices with regard to management, organization, and knowledge.

A major aspect of positivism is the division between object and subject. This means that the outer world (e.g. an industry) is pre-given, ready to be "truthfully" represented by organizations and individuals. The mind is able to create an inner representation that corresponds to the outer world, be it an object, event or state. Translated to knowledge, positivism considers that knowledge exists independent of the human being that uses it, learns it, transfers it. Knowledge reflects and represents "the world in itself" and can be built up independent of the observer, the "knower." This is equally and arguably the basis for most management education today. A student, independent of his/ her background, interest, social environment, ambitions, etc., needs to learn a body of knowledge through courses and is tested on whether that 'objective' knowledge is acquired. Only, the professor who judges is a subject and is involved in the subject matter also. The way one professor teaches is different from the way a colleague teaches and so the content is in fact subject dependent. We call it 'subject matter,' even though we consider it as being an objective set of transferable knowledge. The more companies want to tailor management education to their specific needs based on the pre-knowledge of their employees, the more this positivist object/subject division becomes a problem as it collides with the notion of "universal and objective" knowledge. What if the universal knowledge that is transferred is mainly a theoretical framework, a form which is of little use in the nonlinear and dynamic markets? This would mean management education does not prepare adequately for the managerial reality.

Individualized learning, however, will need an adapted pedagogical approach, which enables dynamic and nonlinear behavior, as is argued in chapter 3. The successful implementation of the concept of the Hybrid Business School is not based on a positivist and reductionist view on management education.

Another premise of positivist thinking is based on a strict belief in (absolute) causality and (environmental) determinism. As there exist clear-cut connections between cause and effect, managerial actions lead to predictable outcomes and thus to control. Successful systems are driven by negative feedback processes toward predictable states of adaptation to the environment. The dynamics of success are therefore assumed to be a tendency towards stability, regularity, and predictability. The classic approach to strategy illustrates this reductionism. The complexities of industries are reduced in terms of maturity, continuity and stability so that a single prediction of an organization's future path can be described. As a consequence, the better the environmental analysis according to a number of dimensions, the better the course (strategy) can be defined and implemented.

Positivism is the prevailing scientific view in the Western world, since it perfectly coincides with the Cartesian view of the world. The overriding power of man is a fact of nature. Nature gives man the power to master nature, according to laws of nature. In 1903 however, Poincaré, a French mathematician, brought some doubt in this positivist view. Without really being able to prove, or even to gather evidence, he warned that "sometimes small differences in the initial conditions generate very large differences in the final phenomena. A slight error in the former could produce a tremendous error in the latter so that prediction becomes impossible; we have accidental phenomena."

It suggested that with the approaches used, man was not always able to control their own systems. Hence, there's the limit to the Cartesian view of the world.

It took quite a number of years until, in 1964, Lorenz showed evidence of the phenomenon. Lorenz, an American meteorologist, was interested in weather forecasting. In order to produce forecasts, he built a simple dynamic nonlinear model. Though it only consisted of a few equations and a few variables, it showed "strange" behavior. A dynamic model is one where the value in a given period is a function of the value in the previous period. For example, the value of a particular price in a given period is a function of its value in the previous period. Or, the market share for product A in a given period is a function of the market share in the previous period. In other words, most if not all, economic phenomena are dynamic. Such a dynamic process that continuously changes can only be simulated by a stepwise procedure of very small increments. It is an iterative process. Once the value of the previous period is calculated, it is used as an input value for the next period, etc.

A computer allowed Lorenz to show what could happen with nonlinear dynamic systems. At a certain moment he interrupted a simulation, since he needed to leave the room suddenly. He requested from the computer a printout of the simulation. When he returned, he decided not to restart the entire simulation from period 0, but rather to start where he had stopped before. Only, in order to be sure, he restarted the simulation a number of periods before. What he observed was remarkable. The new simulation differed increasingly from the one made previously and the differences increased over time. Suddenly, chaos seemed to appear. The observed difference became larger than the signal itself. Hence, the predictive value of the model became zero.

Originally, Lorenz did not understand what happened. He did observe that while the computer calculates with a number of decimal positions, the printout shows less decimal positions. When he started the resimulation, he typed in the value of the output, which was hence slightly different (from the 9th decimal position onwards) from the one the computer really used during the simulations. This very small difference caused chaotic behavior after a number of iterations. Lorenz's observation caused a real paradigm shift in sciences. Lorenz showed what Poincaré suggested, namely that nonlinear dynamic systems are highly sensitive to initial conditions. Complex adaptive systems are probabilistic rather than deterministic, and factors such as nonlinearity can magnify apparently insignificant differences in initial conditions into huge consequences, meaning that the long term outcomes for complex systems are unknowable. Translated to management, this advocates that companies and economies need to be structured to encourage an approach that embraces flux and competition in complex and chaotic contexts rather than a rational one. Mainstream approaches popularized in business texts, however, seldom come to grips with nonlinear phenomena. Instead, they tend to model phenomena as if they were linear in order to make them tractable and controllable, and tend to model aggregate behavior as if it is produced by individual entities which all exhibit average behavior.

One could ask what this has to do with education. The answer is quite simple. Human beings behave and think in a nonlinear and dynamic way. Each individual, even from the same region and benefiting the same pre-education, thinks differently from his or her colleagues. Therefore, one cannot hope that a particular course could fit all students. Further, it is extremely difficult to identify the 'initial condition' of each student. This sensitivity to initial conditions is another reason for investigating new educational paradigms. The old paradigm does not fit the modern world.

Positive feedback has been brought into the realm of economics by Brian Arthur, who claims that there are really two economies, one that functions on the basis of traditional diminishing returns, and one where increasing returns to scale are evident due to positive feedback. Marshall introduced the concept of diminishing returns in 1890. This theory was based on industrial production, where one could choose out of many resources and relatively little knowledge was involved in production. Production then seemed to follow the law of diminishing returns, based on negative feedback in the process and this led to a unique (market) equilibrium. Arthur's second economy includes most knowledge industries. In the knowledge economy, companies should focus on adapting, recognizing patterns, and building webs to amplify positive feedback rather than trying to achieve "optimal" performance. A good example is VHS becoming a market standard, without being technically superior. When video became popular, there were at least two standards on the market, the technically better Betamax and VHS. In the beginning both were present on the market and neither of them was dominant. At a certain point, some video producers chose to make a majority of movies in VHS standard. Obviously, this invited more equipment manufacturers to choose the VHS standard, which in turn invited more movie producers to use the VHS standard. A snowball effect made VHS the market standard, even though Betamax offered better technology at a comparable price.

Brian Arthur also refers to the American political primaries as another example of this 'positive feedback phenomena.' All presidential candidates make a great effort to gain the very first small yet crucial states, such as New Hampshire. It is not because they deliver a lot of votes, but rather because it is known that the candidate who wins these states, will get more campaign funding, more TV time, etc. Those who lose often get into a downward spiral and drop out soon afterwards. American presidents, says Brian Arthur, are not elected by a majority of the American citizens, but rather by those living in a few small states.

Arthur also specified a number of reasons for increasing returns that particularly fits today's economy. As most products, being highly knowledge intensive, with high up-front costs, network effects, and customer relationships, lead to complex behavior. Let us take again the example of Windows. The first copy of Windows is quite expensive due to huge research costs. Microsoft experiences a loss on the first generation. The second and following generations cost very little comparatively, but the revenue per product remains the same. Hence, there is a process of increasing returns.

Two more interesting developments have consequences for our educational practice. Recent neurobiological research, e.g. by Varela, has revealed the concept of self-organization and the concept that knowledge is not stored, but rather created each time over and again, based on the neural capacity of the brain. Cognition is enacted, which means that cognition only exists in action and interpretation. This concept of enacted cognition goes fundamentally against the prevailing idea that things are outside and the brain is inside the person. The subject can be considered as the special experience of oneself, as a process in terms of truth. By identifying with objects, the individual leaves the opportunity for the objects to "talk." In other words, subject and object meet in interaction, in hybrid structures. Individuals thus become builders of facts in constructing contents of knowledge which relate to events, occurences and states. Knowledge is concerned with the way one learns to fix the flow of the world in temporal and spatial terms. Consequently, claims of truth are transposed on objects; the subject is "de-subjectivised." There is not such subdivision between the object and the subject. Cognition is produced by an embodied mind, a mind that is part of a body, sensors and an environment. This issue will reappear in chapter 2 when we focus on the role of managers, or in chapter 5 when we discuss education, and more in particular assessment issues.

Research in artificial life gave us the insight that instead of reducing the complex world to simple simulation models, which are never correct, one could equally define some simple rules, which then produce complex behavior. This is also a form of self-organization, like the flock of birds that flies south. The first bird is not the leader and does not command the flock. Rather, each bird has a simple rule e.g. to stay 20 cm away from its two neighbors. This simple rule allows us to simulate the complex behavior of a flock of birds.

At this stage let us focus on what is understood as complex behavior. Complex systems behavior is the behavior of nonlinear dynamic systems. We talk about a dynamic system if the value in a given period (say today) would depend on the value of the previous period. A nonlinear system is a system in which the evolution of the phenomenon does not take place by adding elements to each period, but rather by multiplying them. Let us give a simple example. Consider water plants on a lake. It is said that in each period, the surface covered by them doubles. That means that each period of time, the surface is multiplied by 2. Over a number of periods t, the surface can be calculated by 2^t. This is an example of both a dynamic system and a nonlinear system. It is dynamic since the surface covered in period t is a function of the surface covered in previous period (times 2). It is nonlinear since in each period, a multiplication takes place and not an addition. This leads to an exponential formula in the end.

Probabilistic, nonlinear dynamic systems are still considered deterministic. That means that such systems follow rules, even if they are difficult to identify and even if the appearance of the simulated phenomenon suggests complete chaos. The same complex system can produce at different times, chaotic or orderly behavior. The change between chaos and order cannot be forecasted, nor can the moment in which it takes places, either in magnitude or direction. Complexity and chaos refer to the state of a system and not to what we commonly know as complicated, i.e. something that is difficult to do. The latter depends not on the system, but more on the environment and boundary conditions. Perhaps for a handicapped person, driving a car is more complicated. In general, building a house seems more complicated than sewing a suit, but for some other people building a house would be less complicated than sewing a suit. This depends on the boundary conditions for each individual person.

To formalize in a simplified way the findings of complexity theory, we could state three characteristics. First, complex systems are highly dependent on the initial state. A slight change in the starting situation can have dramatic consequences in a later period of time caused by the dynamic and iterative character of the system. Second, one cannot forecast the future based on the past. Based on the irreversibility of time principle, one can only take one step ahead at a time, scanning carefully the new starting position. Third, the scaling factor of a nonlinear system causes the appearance of "strange attractors," a local minimum or maximum around which a system seems to stay for a certain period of time in quasi equilibrium. The number of attractors cannot be forecasted, neither can it be forecasted when they attract the phenomenon.

There are myriad insights we gain from complexity theory and its applications in business and markets for management education to better organize the Hybrid Business School around complex markets and behavior. The strength of the self-organizing capacity of the human being and of groups of people forces us to change the focus of education. Instead of school-centered, education becomes learner-centered. The learner decides, chooses and manages based on what he needs for his learning purposes, at that particular moment, and in that particular situation, based on the capacity of that particular individual. The concept of enacted cognition invites us to redefine management education in the direction of learning by doing. Project-based education and competency-based education are two focuses that need to be incorporated in the concept of the Hybrid Business School. The concept of the embodied mind stresses the necessity to learn within a given context. Management education, certainly if organized by a company itself, should be grounded in the corporate effort in knowledge management. One can only learn efficiently within one's own context. Learning is not value free; there is no division between object and subject. Management education can only take place within the managerial context, which is integrated and not separated in functional areas.

The 'irreversibility of time' theorem suggests that there is no best solution. There are "best" principles of which one can learn, but no best solutions or practices that one could copy. There are even no guaranteed solutions that could be used in most circumstances. This fact necessitates a different way of organizing the pedagogical process of learning, once we accept that no theories are universal in management education.

Recent developments within complexity theory suggest that management education should be based on an integrated, holistic approach and not on a reductionist, rationalist paradigm. Many interesting but also difficult challenges arise when management education becomes a useful tool for companies operating in nonlinear dynamic markets. And essentially, this covers all companies. The concept of the Hybrid Business School that we will develop in this book, depicts an approach to the design of a management education and management development approach that supports both companies and managers on an operational level in dynamic and nonlinear markets.

BUILDING BLOCKS FOR THE HYBRID BUSINESS SCHOOL

- The high frequency with which radical and dramatic innovations occur, have created a competitive accelerator and steeper business cycles - making time and speed crucial factors in remaining competitive and forcing companies into quantitative and qualitative leaps of improvement;
- There's a rapid transition from an industrial society into a knowledge society.

REFERENCES

Arthur, B. (1999), Positive Feedbacks in the Economy. Scientific American, February 1999, pp. 92-99.

Christensen, C. (2000), The Innovator's Dilemma. Harper Business.

Cohen, J. & Stewart, I. (1994), The Collapse of Chaos: discovering simplicity in a complex world.

Fingar, P., Aronica, R. and Bryan Maizlish , B. (eds.) (2001), The Death of "e" and the birth of the Real New Economy : Business Models, Technologies and Strategies for the 21st Century. Meghan-Kiffer Press.

McKenna, R. (1997), Real Time. Preparing for the age of the never satisfied customer. Harvard Business School Publishing.

Prigogine, I. and Stengers, I. (1988), Entre le Temps et L'éternité. Fayard.

Van der Linden, G. and Parker, P. (1999), An Exploration of Paradoxes in Managerial and Organizational Complexity: A Postmodern Interpretation of Corporate Vision. In: Baets, W. (ed.) *Complexity and Management, A Collection of Essays, Vol 1*. World Scientific.

Waldrop, M. M. (1992), Complexity. Penguin Books.

Chapter 2

The Corporate Environment

1.   CHANGING MANAGERIAL ROLES AND MANAGEMENT COMPETENCIES

This chapter discusses the impact of new economic realities, the technological revolution and other drivers of change on organizations, organizational processes, and how this impact is consequently translated into the role of managers, managerial processes, and management in general. Further more, we will look into the issue of management competencies. What are management competencies, how are they defined, and what are the important management competencies that can be identified in the context of changing corporate and business environments?

1.1.   Changing Managerial Roles and Mindsets

Companies are girding for more competition and more varied forms of competitive pressure from international, knowledge-rich, and unconventional rivals. Rapid movement into new markets, extreme flexibility, and leveraging the weight of competitors are key. Even organizations in slow-moving industries are suddenly faced with threats from more active and Internet-based competitors. Other companies have seen such drastic changes in their industry's structure that they need to develop a complete new outlook in order to not become obsolete.

A logical starting point is to look into and assess the key factors, which will drive competitive advantage in the future. According to a recent survey of the Economist's Intelligence Unit, companies will have to have a distinct focus on relationships with suppliers and customers, human capital/ human resources, core competencies, capabilities and strategic resources, flexible organizational structures, high productivity, technology and low cost production. These issues will define the hallmark of competitive advantage for the coming ten years, driving firms towards achieving a flexible yet sound strategic strength.

Companies are trying to maximize the leveraging of their core competencies, strategic resources and capabilities by looking to and relying on partners to perform activities in the value chain. Core competencies bundle strategic resources and core technologies, supported by capabilities, and are harmonized in a governing process. They reflect the capacity of creating new businesses, core products, end products and services through the mutation of capabilities and recombinations of resources rather than fixing a few core competencies. Metaphorically pictured as a tree, the root system is core competence, the trunk is core business, the major limbs are core products, and the leaves, flowers, and fruits are end products. The idea of referring to organizations as portfolios of core competencies stresses dispersion and fragmentation. At the same time, firms are looking for new sources of competitive advantage beyond just their core competencies and strategic resources. The diffusion of innovation in the marketplace, the importance of dramatic and radical innovation, and the increasing emphasis on designing new products and moving them to the marketplace rapidly, are other elements that play an important role in this process.

Increasingly, we see the birth of role organizations within a federal model, i.e., networked organizations within a consortium or conglomerate. The Italian fashion company Benetton and the Luxury Brand Gucci are built around such a model. Benetton, for example, is organized around two networks led by strong central authority. One consists of hundreds of small textile firms while the other is based on thousands of retail franchises around the world. Gucci, on the other hand, is a network organization of about seventy small craft firms. Twenty to thirty of them are enabled to join a group of partners on the basis of reliability on quality. Central in Gucci's organization is its buying and cutting department. The company also remains owner of its distribution network.

Indeed, joint ventures, alliances, outsourcing, and cooperation within industries are key to creating such flexible structures. Hence, intense interdependence and demanding expectations are the result. Firms have to establish facilitating, coordinative and cooperative mechanisms in order to promote application and enhancement of its partners' knowledge-intensive competencies. Constantly changing processes, continuously building and rebuilding new capabilities at the heart of competitive edge, the continuous recreation of specific business-related capabilities as well as changing industry structures all bring us to looking at organizations as diverse, de-layered and decentralized, process- and flow-oriented entities. As such, the twenty-first century firms are constantly boundary busting as internal networks overflow external networks and vice versa. This not only makes it difficult to draw clear and objective topological boundaries between an organization and its environment, but the fragmenting impact that they exert prompt people within firms to look at them and their environments as complicated, turbulent, chaotic, antagonistic, complex, and ambiguous realities.

Because of those fragmentations, managers no longer hold a unique position or role in today's organizations. Almost everyone is to be considered a manager in the traditional sense, even the secretary/ executive assistant who must have a sophisticated level of communication and professional skills. Strategic leadership, a traditional role of management role, is much more distributed than ever before. The company's systems are in the hands not of senior executives, but of lower-tier workers. Secretaries or administrative assistants make important decisions concerning with whom their immediate supervisors should communicate, and on what subjects, as there is much information which needs to be intellectually processed for it to all be "important enough" to pass on.

Hence, managers realize increasingly that they are themselves subject and object in/ of these turbulent networks and flows. As a result, they can not escape the complexities with which they are confronted. We're not talking "big" strategic issues, but also the day-to-day occurrences that phenomena managers experience. They turn into paradoxes by which many managers are perplexed. Many of them have the feeling that they are loosing control, that they can no longer "manage over complexity." In the previous chapters, we have tried to come to a deeper understanding of business and organizational life. Moreover, our discussions about complexity have shown that it is impossible to control complexity, as it is a dynamic and nonlinear reality. Hence, we could say that we are at the verge of a new managerial mindset that has to take advantage of the richness of complexity, which concentrates on managing complexities rather than to "manage over complexities."

To illustrate this new managerial mindset or philosophy, we would like to use the analogy with Pirsig's "Zen and the Art of Motorcycle Maintenance." Pirsig describes in much detail and in an approachable way the attitude that we refer to in this book. He argues for openness to the outside world and to the tools with which we work. The book advocates listening to problems and reflecting on possible evidence, rather than using the automatic pilot mechanism that we have developed. It argues strongly against an attitude that has become common in many companies: managers need to know answers to all questions, and if they do not, then they are bad managers. Pirsig, on the other hand, promotes another managerial philosophy, which in many aspects introduces the sufficient conditions for knowledge management. Managers should manage as if they were part of the environment. It is like driving a car. When a person drives a car, he looks at nature through a window. Nature passes by as if the driver was looking at it on a TV screen, while seated in his chair. The driver is not part of the environment. Nature becomes distant and we do not really have any feeling for it anymore. Management becomes a movie that we are watching. On a motorbike, Pirsig argues, the driver is part of nature. He feels and smells nature and is able to react much faster to changes in nature. This analogy suggests that managers should be more in touch with the environment - riding their bike - in order to get a close feeling for how the markets are, how their employees work, and what drives other stakeholders. They should learn and share their experiences rather than stay in their offices, looking outside as if they were looking at a TV screen.

Managers should not operate on automatic pilot, but instead remain attentive to any minor changes that could snowball at a later stage. Self-criticism is a quality that many managers lack, having already "experienced it all". Maybe reality is "slightly" different. Reality hides a dynamic movement that is going to grow very fast. Hence, managers should pay attention to their surroundings and remain alert in order to see. When we have seen, we can start to learn and know.

Instead of overemphasizing procedures and rules, people should be able to have fun in their jobs. Procedures, rules, or processes don't offer the answer. But people who share experiences create knowledge. When people have fun in their jobs, they identify with the job and they put their soul in the job. They are willing to learn and to adapt since they do not feel threatened by rules and regulations. They can come up with an idea or a proposal. They will pay attention to detail since they will observe things they have not seen before and they will enjoy it. Sense for detail is a basic attitude for quality improvement. Furthermore, quality is also the ability to "listen" to issues. By identifying with underlying signifiers, it leaves the opportunity for those signifiers to "talk," to tell their "story." Managers should therefore be attentive by taking time to take critical distance. Let us paraphrase Pirsig in order to make this point clear.

"The motorbike broke down and I knew I had not checked it over carefully enough. I had presumed that it was the rain that had caused the engine to fail. Perhaps what I should have done was just take a step away from the bike, take a good long look at it and attempt to listen to it. Allow it to work on you a while, just the way you would go fishing. You stare at the float and after a while you catch a fish. If you give it the time and the space, and allow it to happen, you will detect some almost imperceptible movement or detail that will attract your attention. And that's what makes the world go round: attention."

If one "listens" to the managerial or organizational phenomenon, often the phenomenon itself suggests solutions. Critical distance and reflection - slowing down the thinking process to become more aware - make individuals think about things, search limitations, and develop an epistemology of inquiry - holding dialogues and developing knowledge about assumptions - that allows them to contribute to the knowledge base by better asking the pertinent questions. Working on management is working on oneself. Quality ends up to be a healthy combination of man and machine. So knowledge management ends up being a healthy combination of a learning culture and an information and knowledge technology based network.

As Pirsig shows, managers should not try to find *the* answer to every issue. Answers to problems about organizational issues only turn into problems about answers. Managerial life, rather, consists of perplexing paradoxes. These paradoxes portray a confusion or collapse of different logical levels. Even though contradictions are inferred, they aren't just referring to a simple contradiction. Paradoxes suppose *con-fusion*: the different levels cannot be confronted because the fusion doesn't negate the differentiation of logical levels. This makes clear why in managerial life the "and ... and" prevails over the "or ... or." It is the "genius of the and" dominating the "tyranny of the or." The answer is not a choice between two elements. "Or" does not lie in two opposing extremes. Travelling between tensions and making use of those tensions allows the search for openings that make new choices possible. That is the "core" competency of the manager. By using and reconciling tensions, by taking critical distance, managers become "agents in realities." Making sense of paradoxes is a powerful vehicle since they portray an intellectual and philosophical context; they say something about the actor, the action and the acting fields. It is in that movement and continuous transformation that paradoxes are expressed.

Management has a clear rhetorical function. It produces new realities, new meaningful contexts with their own particular "grammar." One could say it is the manager's role to identify temporally shared elements within complexity, to identify unity in diversity and diversity in unity while attempting to translate dynamic interactions into the moment. Management of meanings has to be approached as a strategic journey. The manager's interest in meanings and knowledge starts from a time perspective. That's the way to take advantage of the richness of complexity and flux. Knowledge is exactly concerned with what one learns in the process of translating (giving meaning to) the flow of his world and involvement in contexts. Hence, management is a mindset to be understood as a continuous movement without location. It is differing in space and deferring in time.

1.2.   Management Competencies

The fragmented and discontinuous nature of a manager's job and the constant bombardment of information and meetings means that managers don't behave in systematic fashion. It is clear that no single concept of management captures the diversity of roles and activities in which managers are involved. As executives live in and create more complex corporate environments, they will have to master a whole new set of personal skills in order to excel. The need for multifaceted knowledge, intelligence, and competencies necessary to create a flexible strategic vision and the organization's continuous renewal, while being able to preserve the core (building an organization or clock building as Collins and Porras call it) becomes prevalent in management. Competencies reflect the capacity of creating new businesses, core competencies, capabilities, products and services. Great emphasis is placed on the capacity of individuals to learn about the environment, about their performance, their objectives and capabilities, and in light of this learning, to change, and to learn from the change. Indeed, state-of-the-art competencies are sustained through continuous learning, as a genetic sequence of evolutions.

In a broader sense, competencies not only have a relevancy from the standpoint of managerial life, but also have an organizational relevancy. In project-based high-tech firms and flat or networked companies, it is specifically important to increase employability through developing competencies. Increasing employability and personal development is one method of compensating for the lack of vertical promotion.

Which are now the relevant managerial competencies, given the new managerial mindset? Talking about competencies offers a chance to get away from the muddle of traits and motives that are associated with (in this case) a manager's role. Unlike the word "characteristics" which covers anything about the person, "competency" is much more tied to competent performance. In other words, it clearly is role, context, and person related. On the other hand, as Woodruffe previously stated, talking about competencies is like entering a minefield. Numerous lists with "crucial" competencies and myriad competency models are available to the extent that the whole issue of "competency" is an enigma. Competencies have something construed and intangible, something of an illusion. Besides, the term "competency" is used by different people to mean different things. Consequently, different models portray different things.

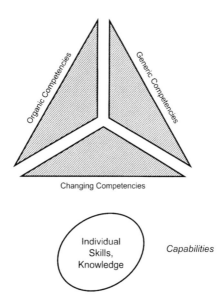

Figure 2-1. Managerial competency model

We think the essence of managerial competencies can be found in the managerial mindset, reflecting an epistemology. An epistemology exactly describes knowledge, wisdom, methods, and their limitations. In analogy with the notion of core competencies, managerial competencies can be seen as bundling strategic resources and intellectual technologies underlying managerial roles and practices, and processes to understand, connect and exploit them in a uniquely competitive way. Specifically the recombination of resources and technologies will be important to managers.

Managerial competencies are supported by capabilities. Capabilities describe for instance the behavioral skills needed to communicate, to work as a member of a team, and to understand the dynamics of the context in which individual managers work. An important personal evolution can thrive through the mutation of capabilities.

In order to portray the different aspects of managerial roles, generic, organic and changing competencies must be differentiated and defined. Once the different competency dimensions are defined, each competency has to be translated in observable, behavioral terms, and must be allocated a relative weight of importance.

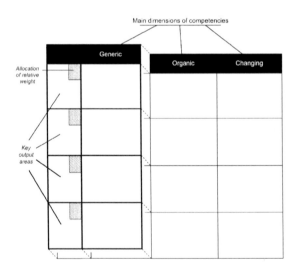

Figure 2-2. Competency table

First we have the "generic" (or transferable) competencies. These competencies are thought to be applicable to an entire class of managers across organizations and specific roles. Existing in all roles across the organization to varying degrees of importance and mastery, they refer to more abstract competencies, to an epistemology of inquiry reflecting thought processes and critical distance that offer continuity. Epistemology is concerned with understanding the origin, nature and validity of knowledge, i.e., the theory of (in this case) inquiry. Generic competencies can be applied by managers in different roles as they reflect the core of the managerial mindset, of managerial and organizational life. Critical distance, making sense of paradoxes, and the ability to "listen" to issues are some of the competencies that would fit in this category. Other examples could include customer-oriented attitude or cross-functional respect. These managers could be described as being open to the customer's changing needs and respectful of the drive, responsibilities and ambitions of colleagues.

Next to these "generic" competencies are the so-called "organic" competencies. Organic competencies arise from a specific job-related role and are therefore role-unique. In a broader sense, one could say they are closely linked and can therefore be derived from a specific company's business strategy, core competencies, capabilities, culture, values, and vision. Managers need to look for patterns that lurk beneath seemingly random behavior and only "organic" competencies can have the specificity and fluidity to represent meaningful categories of specific managerial work or roles and organizational contexts. In that sense, they portray a discontinuity. Technical leadership, issue-solving, and project management are some illustrations of organic competencies.

Third, the "changing competencies" describe a forward-looking approach related to the lifecycle of competencies. As we said earlier, it is crucial not to build from a few competencies, but to recombine resources and technologies; to evolve through the mutation of capabilities. These time-related competencies balance that future, connecting speed to strategic purposes, information, critical issues, and knowledge management. They include emerging, transitional, and maturing competencies: those competencies that have an increasing relevance and importance over the next few years (emerging), the competencies whose relevance are fading out (maturing), or competencies whose relevance may decrease while their emphasis presently remains (transitional). In the first place we tend to think about competencies related to technology as being the changing competencies, due to the constantly changing nature of technology. Another example could include competencies related to business development.

The obvious challenge, then, is how to ensure these competencies are sufficiently embedded in every practice and person of the organization and of the learning process. Sufficiently embedded refers to a consciously learned phenomenon, as opposed to an assumption of innate understanding. Hence, it is concluded that many senior level managers "think" they have excellent leadership and managerial competencies, but have no real medium of measurement. Because it is assumed necessary for all people in a managerial position to have professionally taught leadership, development programs have to ensure that the skills and knowledge are truly alive. Managerial and leadership competencies like networking, visioning, strategic attention for information, among others, all have to support coordination and organizational dynamics, production of tacit knowledge and core capabilities, and consistency with corporate strategies. As we will see later, it requires a complete educational approach to incorporate competencies into development programs. Actually, competencies are one of the important drivers of the alliance between companies and management education providers. As we will see in chapters 5 and 6, the competency approach will be one of the hybrid business school's important elements of added value.

2. INFORMATION AS A DYNAMIC PROCESS

The impact of the new economy on companies and work has been quite complex. The new economy has affected organizational processes and organizational design, the nature of competition, products and services.

Basically the economy has progressed from the industrial age into the information age, from physical sources to knowledge sources. Although physical sources are important aspects of the "value" of the economy, the true value lies in information, learning, and knowledge management. Information and knowledge are presently greatly underestimated and underutilized resources even though the formal process of acquiring and using them effectively is becoming quite obvious.

Let's consider manufacturing in which one can observe a shift from physical resources to information resources. In other words, manufacturing is dematerializing. Think about the beer can, which originally weighed .66 ounces - half the weight of a steel one. Now it weighs about .48 ounces. The gain here is in information, the manufacturing process, information of chemical engineering. Products thrive more on information. More than half the cost of finding and extracting petroleum is information. The BMW 700 series needs more computer power than the Apollo 11 spacecraft that landed on the moon. The value of all chips produced today exceeds the value of steel produced. Market intelligence and information about the customer increasingly become important to increase customer loyalty or to retaining customers. Hence, the new information economy is transforming the old industrial economy and reducing its relative importance.

How do we have to look at information? Is it data that can be stored in databases? The importance of information stems not necessarily from the value and scarcity of information, but rather from the lack of knowledge on how and what information to extract and exploit from the marketplace, as information is (sometimes) free on the market, but not freely accessible or available. A simple example of this is doing a search on the web. Person A enters some key words in his attempt to find needed information (assuming he knows what his optimal information would be for a given situation), and comes up with nothing. Person B enters his key words, and soon has all the information he thinks he needs. Person B has an "information" advantage.

Information's price does not reflect its value. That is, the usefulness, and the value of information are intertwined. Particular information is useful to one person in one particular context, because it has a particular meaning. That doesn't mean that for another person that same information will have the same meaning or usefulness, hence for that person it has a different value or price. The well-known Sabre system that provides information about travelers is a good example. American Airlines, the owner of the system, sells the information gathered via the system to many companies who use the information for various reasons.

Furthermore, information and its nature are changing rapidly as a result of the collapse of time and space. Information can be looked at from a different perspective as technology creates more accessibility. As certain information becomes less scarce or less accurate, it becomes less valuable, therefore its nature changes. For example, through the Internet the layman can now freely access stock quotes from the world's largest markets at any time of the day. This makes brokers more exposed as they no longer possess scarce information, but only the knowledge on how to use that information. The fact that an investor can now get the information in real time has led many to cut out the broker and attempt to manage and trade his own portfolio. As a result, brokers will have to develop a different information base in order to show or recreate their added value.

As information is continually in flux, its meaning, relevance and value are constantly slipping beyond grasp. Information is produced, anchored, and embedded in networks connecting signifiers and meaningful nods (issues). These networks can be imagined as rich webs of meanings with dynamic interactions and knowledge creation between multiple actors, only having a temporal meaning and gathering that temporal meaning in relation to a particular context. Hence, information has to be regarded as a dynamic process. As we showed earlier, turbulent interactions with and between different stakeholders of a corporation prove that the complexity of the business, organizational and management environments cannot be reflected by one or a couple of variables. The essence of complexity is defined by the lack of linearity and fixed causalities.

The corporate world does not really refer to information in dynamic terms. Consider for instance Human Resource Management Information Systems (HRIS), which are designed to help organize myriad administrative and strategic variables of which the Human Resources department is responsible. Starting from a given model or template of generic "common best practices," information about payroll integration, worldwide tax administration, expatriate administration, tracking global assignments, recruiting employees, planning careers and successions, monitoring health and safety, compensation and benefits administration, training and development administration, is all stored in predefined databases. This example shows the rather rigid and static approach of information. Dynamism is translated in the manual updating of the information stored within the databases, or by redefining the links between the different databases.

The impact of understanding information as a dynamic process can be illustrated by two examples. To start, we take Christodoulou's example of a simulation, using variable structures in order to handle complex situations.

Dynamic simulations are increasingly used as a strategic exploration tool, as they address the shortcomings of static analyses that most established frameworks offer. The following table summarizes and compares some of the widely used strategic analysis frameworks. They share the characteristic that they are static in nature.

Specifically, the most widely used framework for modelling and analyzing competitive industry dynamics is Porter's Five Forces model. The structure-conduct-performance paradigm upon which Porter's five forces is based, assumes that each player adopts a single, well-defined and unchanging role. In addition, it only assumes that industry structure is fixed, only considering differences in average industry profitability without taking into account rivals' choices as to whether to compete or not. Game theory models strategic decisions and offers valuable insight on matters of competition and bargaining but addresses the issue of dynamic situations through a collection of static equilibria. In addition, game theory assumes optimal behavior and perfect rationality on the part of the players.

Table 2-1. Strategic Analysis Frameworks

	Five Forces	*Core Competence*	*Game Theory*
Assumptions	Stable industry structure	Firm as a bundle of competencies	Industry as a dynamic oligopoly
Goal	Defend position	Sustain advantage	Temporary advantage
Performance Driver	Industry structure	Unique firm competencies	Right 'strategies' (moves)
Strategy	Pick an industry, a strategic position, fit organisation	Create a vision, build and exploit competencies	Make right competitive and co-operative moves
Success	Profits	Long term dominance	Short-term win

Actual human decision-making, however, is often far from optimal and perfectly rational. Given the highly dynamic markets that firms inhabit today, the problem we face is how to model and simulate markets and economic systems that exhibit a particularly complex behaviour. The aim is to model the evolution of a market and its participants over time, to gain a deeper understanding of how the market under consideration works, and finally, learn how best to manage change.

Forrester's System Dynamics (SD) and Ninios's OO/DEVS are two of the more traditional platforms used for strategic business simulations. Their focus is primarily on the dynamic behavior that results from a given market structure. Once the structure and policy rules have been defined, the model will describe the dynamic behavior of the system, but system components and relations among components do not vary. The model might accurately capture the structure of a complex system, but this will only be valid for as long as the current taxonomy holds and remains unchanged. In other words, fixed structure models cannot anticipate and cannot account for changes that might occur in the composition of the system, leading to incorrect causal relations and models that need to be reformulated.

Simulations based on theories of artificial life, as were also described in a previous section, embrace the idea that aggregate behavior cannot be thought of as simply being the sum of behaviors of 'average' individuals. In addition, the taxonomy of the system studied should not remain fixed, but should have the ability to evolve over time. The complex systems one should be studying can be defined as a set of simple, heterogeneous, interacting agents capable of exchanging information with their environment and capable of adapting their internal structure as a consequence of this interaction. The behaviour of the (economic) agents at the micro level could bring changes at the aggregate market level and, more importantly, new agents can, if appropriate, enter the market.

The motivation for this approach is to model industries and markets that can endogenously change their own structure. This is achieved by treating individual players as agents and providing the means for entry and exit of economic agents in a system (say a marketplace) as well as exchange of information among them. Our concern is not to consider the states that will finally emerge, but rather to describe the original system, to ascertain how agents act and react to current circumstances and thus understand the actual process of market evolution and the role that economic agents play in defining these changing structures. We aim to explore industries and markets where we have a multiplicity of actors that individually make assumptions about what will happen in the market and, as a result, bring about changes both at the individual (firm) and at the aggregate (market) level of observation. One thus aims to understand economic organization as a dynamic, adaptive process of interactions among individuals ('agents') in realistic and complex environments. This sort of models offer a useful way of looking at how market structure and organization emerge.

The 'structural limitations' of traditional modelling and simulation techniques are thus addressed and the issue of changing industry structure by considering how the economic agents' behavior can alter the structure of a system is explored, as shown in the figure below. This figure shows how one attempts to close the existing gap caused by a static approach in business simulations, by moving from dynamic behavior to dynamic structure.

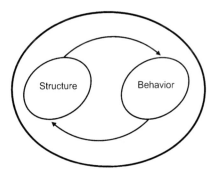

Figure 2-3. From dynamic behavior to dynamic structure

By doing this, one can understand market dynamics at the population level by considering the actions and interactions of individual agents. One can also look at dynamic models of endogenous mergers and acquisitions, investment, entry and exit using descriptive models based on decentralized agents whose collective interactions produce emergent behavior.

This approach perfectly fits the complexity theory where the initial conditions of the system and the dynamic development path describe a system. From an ICT point of view, we propose an object oriented framework that allows for changing model structure. In other words, a model could dynamically adapt its structure during a simulation run when necessary. Economic agents are objects (in object oriented programming terms) that interact with other agents through a series of messages. Each of them has a series of attributes and procedural methods with which it accomplishes things. The agents of the system do not simply react to external messages and data, but given the 'knowledge' they have they can act as evolving, interrelated entities with the capability of changing their own environment.

This approach creates a tool for building models that can dynamically change their structure and can thus study a range of interesting managerial problems. This methodology can therefore be used as a learning tool, where management teams can model and test their assumptions and explore some of the possible futures. It is not meant to provide exact forecasts or make any statements about the probability of different outcomes.

Our second example using Artificial Neural Networks (equally described in the previous section) for building complex adaptive systems, carries the same idea a step further. Neural networks are trained in the first place via a number of experiences. The neural network (which is a piece of software) attempts to learn patterns, in such a way, that it can reproduce all the cases that it learned. But once a neural network has learned this capacity to reproduce cases, it can equally reproduce new cases that it never saw before.

Neural networks show a remarkable capacity to continuously learn. They learn from each new experience. Building the information system never stops. Such systems can guide people through an information base, or through a learning environment, based on their preferences, pre-knowledge, experience, etc. The changing personal development path automatically offers the employee the adapted learning material for the new career move that is planned, or provides the corporate applications on the theoretical course followed the previous week. An evaluation system connected to such a learning environment feeds back into the personal development path and in a continuous interaction dynamically adapts both the personal development path and the individualized learning environment. At a later stage, when we look more deeply into the link between virtual learning and knowledge management (what we will call the Hybrid Business School) these links will prove to be a distinctive value added to the proposed approach.

The same perspective is used while building knowledge-based approaches for identifying client profiles. One can construct a particular information system that will only partly describe reality. It generates client profiles at a particular moment, for a particular market. The process of using the information systems continuously with both the existing and new clients and markets creates new information that in turn allows the information system to learn and adapt. Such complex adaptive systems show the dynamic behavior that is strived for today, but another focus on information systems is needed as well. The concept of the Hybrid Business School, as developed in this book, fits this focus of information as a dynamic process, where the learner creates as much as he or she consumes.

3. KNOWLEDGE AND LEARNING

3.1. Knowledge and Experience

In cognitive sciences and even more so in epistemology a great deal of research and work has been done to attempt to identify and define knowledge. Unfortunately, in management, we do not know what managerial knowledge really is and even though we have a vague feeling for it, there are few definitions of knowledge within a "managerial" context.

Kim suggested that knowledge is a combination of "know-how" and "know-why." Other authors, including Nonaka, identify different types of knowledge, i.e., tacit and explicit knowledge. Explicit knowledge, on the one hand, refers to the formal, systematic language, the rules and procedures that an organization follows. This kind of knowledge can be transferred and therefore can be a subject of education and socialization. Knowledge-based systems also work with explicit knowledge. Tacit knowledge, on the other hand, is mainly based on lived experiences and therefore is difficult to identify and to transfer. Deeply rooted in action, commitment and involvement in a specific context, it refers to personal qualities such as cognitive and technical elements inherent to the individual.

Experience is key in acquiring tacit knowledge. An example of tacit knowledge (in business) would be the decision making process of financial markets dealers. Based on what they have learned from their past experience, what they read and hear, the "climate on the market," etc., brokers make decisions on buying and selling within a few seconds. We like to call this "instinct" or "fingerspitzengefuhl" but the behavior of individual dealers is different. Each individual dealer seems to have his own way of dealing based on his experience and his reference framework. It has proven extremely difficult to extract this kind of "knowledge" from dealers but not because they don't want to share it. Rather, it seems extremely difficult for dealers to express their knowledge, or to make tacit knowledge explicit. However, since some dealers are consistently better than others, it would be interesting to understand why they excel, in order to reproduce the principles of "winning" behavior. Furthermore, if a dealer acquires his experience/knowledge during his stay in a particular bank company, how can this bank keep the acquired knowledge, this intangible asset or human capital, if a dealer leaves the company? Intangibles, as the embodiment of knowledge and ideas, are what drive growth in an information economy. Taken together, intangibles comprise well over half the market value of public companies, and can entail, besides human capital, organizational capital including intellectual property and brands, customer capital, partner capital, and environmental capital.

Many different types of cognitive elements are involved. Those of interest for managerial problems center on "mental models" in which people form working models of the world by creating and manipulating analogies in their minds. Mental models could be described as deeply held images of how the world works. They represent a person's view of the world, including explicit and implicit understanding. Mental models provide the context in which to view and interpret new material and they determine how stored information is relevant to a given situation. There's a clear analogy between how mental models "work" and the way in which the human brain works. The human brain is characterized by a high degree of parallelism. This means that a large number of elements (in this case neurons) are used at the same time alongside each other. A second important characteristic of the human brain is the micro structure of cognition (distributed knowledge) on which it is built. The human brain has no clear equation for what happens in a given situation, but is able to reconstruct solutions and actions, quickly and easily, based on this micro structure of knowledge. Consequently, we can assume that knowledge is not sequential (but parallel) and deals with variety (and not with averages).

Based on these definitions and analogies to individual learning, organizational learning is defined as increasing an organization's capacity to take effective action. The emphasis doesn't lie on reality but rather on perceptions of reality (meanings). It is clear from this description how crucially important context is for learning and knowledge.

The capacity of an organization to take effective action is based on tacit corporate knowledge. The more this corporate knowledge is accessible (which does not necessarily mean explicit) and shared, the easier it becomes to take advantage of it. For management, perceptions of reality become more important than reality itself. Hence the role of corporate mental models becomes extremely important since their ultimate aim is to visualize the shared mental model on any chosen subject. A shared mental model is fundamental to corporate learning, and hence to proactive management. If one wants to take this reasoning one step further, one could even consider that it is the manager's role to identify the shared elements or unity within diversity (complexity). This idea introduces management of corporate (tacit) knowledge as a strategic mission.

The idea of unity within diversity also advocates that organizations are most creative when they operate away from equilibrium, in a region of "creative tension." This involves thinking about the fractal nature of organizational boundaries and the realization that all employees are at some boundary of their organizations, and therefore understand part of their firm's environment. Instead of absorbing complexity, diversity and therefore uncertainty, creative tension gives rise to the richness as it embraces advancement and creativity. According to Nonaka, such "creative chaos" may need to be intentionally created by management through an organization, and allow for self-organization processes. If managers are not allowed time for reflection during this time, creative chaos can become "destructive chaos." As a consequence, redundancy should be built into managerial structures and processes.

Despite the variety of definitions, the organizational capability for knowledge creation is gaining momentum in managerial science. Some consider it a potential source of competitive advantage for companies. The organizational competency translating all that information and knowledge into "intelligence," in other words to understand, connect, an exploit those resources in a distinctive competitive way, however, is crucial. Whereas companies have long been dominated by a paradigm that conceptualizes the organization as a system that "processes" information and/or "solves" problems, we now consider an organization as a knowledge creating system. The dynamic nature, the continuous change, and the discontinuous leaps such a system lives through, are essential. In order to describe a company's pool of knowledge, some authors use the metaphor of a "cognitive map," a written plan in which a person expresses, via blocks and connecting arrows, how a person reasons about a particular subject or how s/he sees "things" fit together. In a similar vein, the term "corporate IQ" is sometimes used while others argue for a more quantitative representation of this "body" and call it a "fusion map." In essence, all describe in one way or the other this portfolio or repository of (tacit and explicit) knowledge.

3.2. Learning and Mental Models

Learning could then be considered as advancement. It represents an opportunity for individuals to pause, reflect upon and reframe issues and experiences not only from their own insights, but also in the interaction with others. Hence, learning is not abstract but contextual: it happens at the appropriate time, in the appropriate dose with the proper experience so that it can be immediately applied. As such, learning can be seen as the process whereby knowledge is created through the transformation of experience.

This definition of learning relates to Kim's "know-how" and "know-why." According to this definition, learning takes place in a cycle of four steps. First something is experienced within a particular context. Second, observations and reflections on that experience are created. Third, abstract concepts and generalizations are formed based on these reflections, and fourth, these ideas on the new situation are tested which in turn result in new experiences. These new experiences can then become a first step in a new loop.

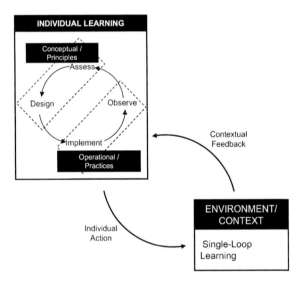

Figure 2-4. Simple model of Individual Learning - the OADI-cycle

The idea of a cyclical learning loop is described in the so-called OADI-cycle (Observe - Assess - Design - Implement).

An easy example of this learning process is to observe how a child "learns" not to put his hand on a hot plate. In many cases, a child cannot be taught not to touch a hot plate. The first time (even if told differently) a child attempts to touch a hot plate. The child observes something that he assesses as heat. He designs, not necessarily deliberately, an action which is probably to take away his hand. Eventually, the child implements that design and does take away his hand. A new observation follows which is assessed as "better." Probably no further design takes place. In the case of the hand having been burned already, the child again observes something different which does not feel very nice. He would (or in the beginning somebody else would) assess it as "burned." A possible design would be to put his hand under cold running water, which he eventually does. The cycle can continue for a number of rounds. Via this process of "learning the hard way," an individual, regardless of age, learns a number of things through experience. Learning is inseparable from "taking action" and it applies knowledge to events. The nature of that knowledge includes not only explicit, but also implicit understanding and meaning that the individual ascribes to events and their purposes. The single-loop process is implemented through individual action, which in turn creates a contextual feedback. Instruction can shorten the learning cycle, but only if the person can make sense of it. This means that the instruction given should fit into the existing reference frame of the person. As a result, instruction without embedding - contextualization - has limited value added.

A second stage of individual learning links individual learning with individual mental models. This process is called double loop learning as it includes learning based on contextual impulses as portrayed by the OADI-cycle as well as learning from connecting what is learned from impulses with the individual's mental models.

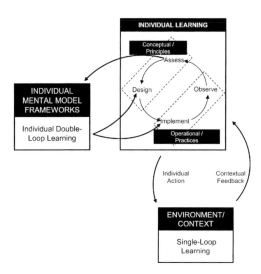

Figure 2-5. Individual Double-Loop Learning

Let us take the illustration of the child again. When a child goes through the above-mentioned "experience" a number of times, he will not do it again.

The child does not necessarily know what happens and he does not necessarily understand why he should not touch a hot plate anymore. He has implicitly developed a framework of knowledge that allows him to deal with a new comparable case. He can deal with a new case, without knowing the correct "equations." In some respects it can be argued that this is not a true example of learning, but rather of a human reflex. Probably this is true, however, it indicates clearly how the learning cycle operates in contextual interaction (single-loop learning) and how it leads to the individual mental model (via individual double-loop learning). According to the same principle, the trader "learns" and creates by doing, his own mental model about trading. Any learning experience (courses, or books read) could speed up the process, if and only if the experiences fit into the existing framework (mental model) of the person. If the gap between the existing mental model and the taught material is too large, very little learning takes place. Teaching is no guarantee for learning: teaching is only one kind of experience that an individual can choose to use for learning purposes and ultimately from which to learn. Field experience can be another means or medium of learning. Hence, different people react completely differently to the same learning experience. No unique best way of teaching exists, no unique best way of learning can be identified. Learning remains a free act of individuals.

We will now add a comparable double-loop learning model on an organizational level, in two different ways. Comparable to the single-loop learning in the individual model, each individual action can be part of an organizational action, which in turn causes additional contextual feedback. This is called organizational single-loop learning. Organizational double-loop learning takes place when the individual mental models (images, meanings) are brought together in order to form shared mental models (shared on a corporate or group level), which in turn have an influence on the individual mental models. It is in surfacing and questioning tacit knowledge that it is possible, by a process of "dialoguing," to create shared meanings, which build a sense of identity and purpose with which individuals in organizations can identify. In figure 2-6, shared mental models are also defined as organizational routines. It will especially be these explicit shared models (the explicit organizational routines) that enable the learning ability of an organization.

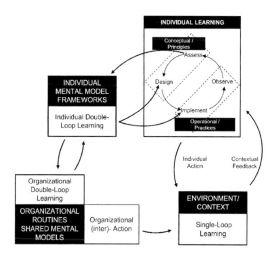

Figure 2-6. Organizational Double-Loop Learning

Organizational double-loop learning can only take place by bringing together individual mental models in a learning space. Individual mental models only get created through individual learning experiences. One particular experience doesn't have a direct impact, either on the individual mental models or on the shared mental models. In other words, there's no fixed causality between the two. Any change in the shared mental model is caused by individual experiences, which in turn changes the individual mental models and only then would a new shared learning activity be able to change a shared mental model. This does not mean that shared mental models are an addition to individual mental models, or that they are only the addition of a number of individual mental models. On the contrary, any attempt to change a shared mental model has to happen through new experiences at the individual level (even if these experiences can take place in teams or groups). As an individual learns, inferring that he fits the new experience into his mental model and produces a different mental model, some changes can occur on the shared level. However, it remains almost impossible to foresee the impact on the shared model of any action on the individual's level, before it comes via the individual mental model into the shared mental model. Therefore, a shared mental model is not a static entity. It should be monitored continuously and that is what we understand as picturing and comparing mental models.

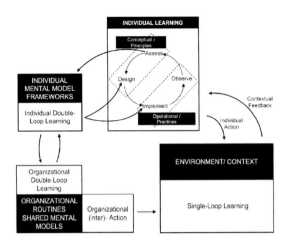

Figure 2-7. An Integrated Model of Organizational Learning

Knowledge management in this sense attempts to visualize mental models with the aim of learning from them and sharing them. As we have seen earlier, business is not only faster but also fundamentally different: it moves in a nonlinear and unpredictable fashion. The trouble comes in figuring out how all the forces and elements interact to shape an overall system and determine its often surprising outcomes. As there is no continuity in the flow of (competitive) events, and there is no way to predict the success of products or companies, analytically driven strategies and shaping the organization to meet the needs of the business are obsolete. Without the adequate knowledge base, knowledge management and the organizational capability to continuously capture information, generate new ideas and put knowledge into practice, it is difficult for companies to emerge from the changing economic realities. And information is not just data, knowledge not just codification, but rather the gathering of patterns, the bundling of strategic resources and intellectual technologies, and processes to understand, connect and exploit them in a uniquely competitive way. Hence, organizations have to become learning organizations. Besides, the knowledge-creating and learning organization perspectives touch all of the assumptions underlying the organization's structures and processes, and changes the roles, responsibilities, competencies and activities of all involved, and especially the roles of managers. Organizational learning magnifies and closes the loop of individual learning within a dynamic corporate and networked setting that allows the learning process inside a company to excel beyond efficiency frontiers. The organization's capabilities, everything from resources, infrastructures and support systems to enabling constraints and core philosophy, will drive that organizational learning. But inherently, we're talking simple cognitive processes.

The most famous example of how a shared mental model differs from the addition of a number of individual mental models is no doubt the one of the cage of monkeys and the bananas. If one puts twenty monkeys into a cage with a step in the middle and a bunch of bananas on the top, the smartest monkey runs up the steps and takes a banana. This monkey follows its "individual mental model." This story is mainly used as a metaphor, and it is not argued here that monkeys have a mental model. Next, when the monkey takes the banana it starts to rain. Monkeys don't like rain. Then, one monkey is taken out of the cage and replaced. The second smartest monkey runs up the step, and following its mental model takes the banana. It rains again. Allow us to draw your attention to the fact that each monkey individually feels the rain, which gradually influences its mental model in that respect. Again a monkey is replaced. This story continues until the smart monkeys have understood the mechanism. Individually they still like the bananas but they understand the consequences. The least intelligent monkey then tries to take a banana. That monkey has not understood the mechanism yet. Again it pours and we again change a monkey. The new monkey will try and run up the step. All the others, having understood, will not try anymore. But all the monkeys in the cage will also try to stop the new monkey from taking a banana. The new monkey does not understand, but he cannot get to the banana. He follows the shared behavior without understanding. Another twenty replacements will be delivered to a cage full of monkeys that all individually would like to take the banana. As a group they do not do that and none of them knows why. The shared mental model is clearly different from the individual mental models. The change has taken place via continuous new observations and experiences which all the monkeys had individually. None of them has the same number of experiences since they were replaced at different times.

This story illustrates the learning process and also shows that a shared mental model can be completely different from the sum of the individual mental models. Change in a shared mental model only occurs via experiences on an individual level, influencing the individual mental model first. The latter, in turn, will influence the shared mental model. How many times do we recognize this in a corporate environment? "Why do we do it this or that way?" Answer: "It's the way we've always done it." Nobody necessarily knows why and the individual models could well differ from the shared one. Is this what we call "corporate culture"?

If we would like to change corporate culture, we cannot dictate the change process as it is nonlinear and emergent. Actions have to be undertaken in order that all individuals get new experiences. If the atmosphere is positive enough around these new experiences, individuals may - but cannot be forced to - integrate these new positive experiences into their individual mental models, which in turn, eventually, could change the shared model (i.e. the culture). It is a long process, which occurs through individual learning.

Management education can be seen as an important vehicle in developing "emergent" strategies, knowledge management and the organization's capabilities that drive organizational learning. It can help in creating the right conditions for reflective thinking and learning. Referring to figure 2-7, management education could be situated in the area for single-loop learning. As the figure shows, there is an important role for the context (of which a business school can be part) to give input to the learning process of individuals and groups. However, learning takes place in the double-loop parts and if it did not take place, management education as an input to this process would be a waste of effort.

It is crucial, therefore, that management education and knowledge management be harmonized. They mutually are in need of and reinforce each other. Due to the existence of information technology, both can be easily integrated, resulting in a virtual business school. Technology, however, is only a medium. A context including a pedagogical approach to the corporate learning and knowledge process has still to be provided. Therefore, a virtual business school needs to include these ingredients incrementally in order to be successful. First, an adequate pedagogical approach and an appropriate mix of management education and knowledge management are crucial. Further, the company is required to think about a specific knowledge and learning approach and must have a strong belief and commitment to link management education with knowledge management. Learning and knowledge processes are not static, however, as they are built on information as a dynamic process, working with a dynamic network of human interactions. Last, the appropriate information technology has to be used in order to support the educational side, the knowledge side and communication.

After this extensive introduction to knowledge and learning, we should now position clearly the role of virtual education. From a corporate point of view, management education comes into the picture in the single-loop learning cycle, but only to the extent that it fits with the corporate knowledge approach. Management education, and particularly the use of ICT in management education, creates added value if it can be joined with the corporate effort to manage knowledge. Management education can introduce concepts, cases, and activities, but it really becomes interesting if these are taken further in a double-loop learning process via a knowledge approach (or a knowledge network).

Based on IT, the virtual business school is a perfect place for single-loop learning, transfer of contextual knowledge and creation of contextual input for learning. Management education needs to be a stimulus for further in-company learning, further mental model building and further shared mental model building. Business schools can play an important role here, if there is close cooperation with companies. When companies set up their own "corporate" universities, it is because they are not satisfied with the (too generic) offerings of management institutes, the way management education fits their internal efforts, as well as cost issues among others. But if companies set up their own "corporate university" in order to organize the transfer of external knowledge, they run a big risk to make a kind of a clone of their own knowledge system (provided they have one). Or, instead of creating a university, they run the risk rather to create a knowledge sharing system. There is nothing wrong with this, but it is not a business school.

The most likely evolution is that business schools will offer knowledge to companies in a flexible, hybrid way (using technology). This fits the virtual business school approach combined with the companies' own knowledge management effort. Ideally, business schools and companies will cooperate in the implementation of the overall concept of virtual education and knowledge management. The more closely the bases of management education and the knowledge base are, the more value it will add to the company. Business schools must consequently organize their "material" differently, feeding into the knowledge networks as we will discuss further.

As already argued in the introduction, university administrators and faculty will need to be flexible. This evolution changes the role of the university and the faculty; it could even change its status. If we want to imbed knowledge-creating processes using management education in order to manage the overall complexity of companies and management, we must put more emphasis on mindsets, learning and knowledge, both in the management education part and the company itself. This fact will affect both approaches and structures (architectures) of companies. There is still a long way to go in this respect. Joint efforts and developments among artificial intelligence, cognitive sciences, and modern human resources management (i.e. more strategic versus pure administrative and operational) will enhance knowledge management in a business environment. Organizational learning will evolve as well by this cooperation. Above all, however, business schools and companies should start cooperating on the implementation and deployment of integrated knowledge networks/virtual learning platforms.

BUILDING BLOCKS FOR THE HYBRID BUSINESS SCHOOL

- Information is a dynamic process. Knowledge is concerned with the way one learns to fix the flow of the world in temporal and spatial terms;
- Business, markets, and organizations change in a discontinuous, nonlinear and dynamic way, allowing for the possibility of emergent and self-organizing behavior. Emergence cannot be predicted or even "envisioned" from the knowledge of what each component of a system does;
- No single concept of management captures the diversity of roles and activities in which managers are involved;
- The capacity of an organization to take effective action is based on tacit corporate knowledge. Knowledge management attempts to visualize that tacit knowledge to learn from it and share it;
- Managerial competencies better portray the particularities of managerial roles. Managerial competencies are sustained through continuous learning.

REFERENCES

Baets, W. (1998), Organizational Learning and Knowledge Technologies in a Dynamic Environment. Kluwer Academic Publishers.

Collins, J. (2001), Good to Great: Why Some Companies Make the Leap... and Others Don't. Harper Collins.

Christodoulou, K. (1998), Modelling and simulation of variable structure systems: a way to handle complexity. In: Baets, W. (ed.) *Complexity and Management. A collection of essays, vol. 1.* World Scientific.

Economist Intelligence Unit (1997), Vision 2010. Designing tomorrow's organization. The Economist Intelligence Unit.

Hamel, G. (2002), Leading the Revolution: How to Thrive in Turbulent Times by Making Innovation a Way of Life. Plume.

Kim, D. (1993), The Link Between Individual and Organizational Learning. Sloan Management Review, Fall 1993.

Nonaka, I. And Takeuchi, H. (1995), The Knowledge-Creating Company: How Japanese Companies Create the Dynamics of Innovation. Offord University Press.

Pirsig, R. (1974), Zen and the Art of Motorcycle Maintenance. Penguin Books.

Woodruffe, C. (1991), Competent by any other name. Personnel Management, September, pp. 30-33.

Chapter 3

The Business Education Environment

As we have established in the previous chapters, managerial roles have changed and are changing in nature. Logically, therefore, relevant managerial competencies must also change over time, and it is necessary to discuss changing managerial competencies. Not surprisingly, managerial competencies and/ or the lack thereof, are a main topic of criticism from the business as well as the business school communities.

1. CRITICISMS FROM BUSINESS ON BUSINESS SCHOOLS

The main criticism surrounding business education stems from a lack of "cleverness" in business and management graduates, leading us to believe that the "problem" lies not in the specific curriculum per se, but rather in the educational approach. Some authors already have come to the conclusion that business education is not preparing students for the challenge of corporate life, as it probably emphasizes the wrong model of management education. Literature also echoes that the dominant paradigm of management education is not entirely relevant to the needs of graduates, and hence does not prepare them for their managerial roles. Research, in the form of literature or executive interviews, not surprisingly, reveals several "categories" of criticism of management education. For the purpose of making a point, however, we will generalize in our categorization. The first category refers to "too much"; the second refers to "too little."

A main criticism refers to a too great focus on the transfer of "best past practices." Given the specificity of each individual company coupled with turbulence and complexity in which they operate, education must focus more succinctly on "best principles" rather than "best practices." As every manager knows, blueprint answers to blueprint questions are rarely effective. Practices must be brought back to a more conceptual level of principles, where a challenge can be studied and where an answer can be sought. Principles can then be translated to a specific context at some point in the future. It is in this ability of playing between levels that a manager's strength lies.

Another important factor is that principles do change over time. Principles are more easily adaptable than practices, which are far more rigid. Working with principles also teaches participants to develop a conceptual reading and cohesive mindset about management and a theory of practice, providing them with broader powers of strategic analysis. But how many students and participants can really translate a managerial phenomenon to a conceptual level, come to an understanding by asking pertinent questions, and translate that understanding back to a practical level? Where is that critical distance?

Again on the "abundance" side, there's too much storytelling going on in business schools. Too much anecdotal information is given, lacking deeper conceptual ground or clear relevancy. Graduates go (back to) their companies with all sorts of stories (often heroic), without really knowing how they relate to any specific challenge they face. Linked to this, there's too much emphasis on transfer of knowledge rather than transfer of learning. Acquiring knowledge is one thing, but learning to learn, whether it be continuous development or learning from a particular situation or issue and how to use that later on, is quite another. The ideal understanding of "a career" as a sequence of learning and development experiences is neither really established in MBA or MBA-type programs nor in more traditional programs.

A large percentage of management programs are too functional and discipline-oriented. This is based on an approach to management and business as a "learned" profession. An important element of this "professionalization" of business programs is the insistence on a division of subject matter into categories (functional areas or domains) that have their separate conceptual bases, as opposed to an interdisciplinary and multidisciplinary complexity with a common ground. Advocates of this "professional" approach claim that one can only truly understand the overall picture and become more efficient in one's decision-making through compartmentalization.

In most business-type programs, however, it is up to the participants to put the pieces of the overall puzzle in place, that is, to understand how the different "classes" relate to a unified whole "program." One can wonder how many students actually do so without the proper guidance, or in other words, can really understand management by compartmentalization. Looking at MBA students engage in a business simulation in which they "run" a mock company, where they must take into account the dynamics between different functional areas and between economic drivers, only a minority succeeds. As expected, most players focus on the different functional areas of the company one at a time, not going beyond the trivial and obvious. They practice analytical detachment over integrative insight, which proves that management is more than the sum of its parts.

Like the functional and discipline-oriented approach, the rational quantitative as opposed to the qualitative approach is overstressed in business programs. For example, when looking at management in terms of complexity and flux, a qualitative approach would bring in added value. The richness of managerial life and business cannot just be solely translated in figures, but requires - as every manager knows - a more qualitative approach. And even when dealing with figures, a qualitative assessment of these figures is needed. Qualitative methods, like mind mapping and decision-making techniques, can bring an insight in managing complexity, rather than managing over complexity which is embedded in a pure quantitative approach. The manager, however, is not able to control the increasing complexity of organizational life by overlaying a template of pure functional rationality.

Executives also criticize business institutions for having too much of a focus on technical problem solving in which problems are found, isolated, and then "clinically" analyzed. This is what we could call the engineering or technocratic approach to management. Inherently, there's an overemphasis on cognitive learning which focuses on theories, models and facts. This approach gives students the impression that there has to be an answer - *the* answer - to every problem. In other words, management problems can be fitted in to neat, narrowly specialized technical packages. As explained earlier, however, the strength of a manager lies in asking of pertinent and relevant questions, and in taking advantage of the richness of complexities and turbulence to guide him in his problem-solving. Because in reality, in managerial life the "and ... and" must prevail over the "or ... or:" the "genius of the and" dominating the "tyranny of the or." There is no such thing as *the* answer, and it is too limiting to even think in those terms. Travelling between tensions or extremes and making use of those tensions and contradictions allows the search for openings that make new choices possible. That is one of today's managerial "core" competency boundaries.

We would like to start our second category of criticism - the "too littles" - by pointing out a serious lack of cross-cultural awareness in most business programs. Cultural awareness and academically based cross-cultural courses seem to be more of a small detail for most institutions and programs. A one-day seminar on cross-cultural management or working in groups with participants from different countries throughout the program is a common approach to integrating cross-cultural skills. This has proven time and again not to be enough. When we question how many faculty members have truly international experience, or have worked in different countries and experienced different management styles, we find out that the percentage is very low. We must question to what extent professors are aware of cultural biases and assumptions in management models, concepts, techniques or theories and if it is enough to explain those biases to students and participants? Therefore, a real international scope lacks in many programs.

In addition to too little cross-cultural awareness being embedded into programs, there is also too little future-orientation in many business programs. Often, outdated models and theories are still commonly taught. Most of the strategic concepts that are still used, for example, are those developed in the 1920s. New and innovative concepts based on new economies, changing business and organizational processes and the new roles of managers are rarely touched upon. For example, how many programs include seminars or courses on the application of complexity and chaos theory to change management, manufacturing or economy? The disadvantage of focusing on leading-edge ideas, however, is that the corporate world even has yet to embrace them. At any rate, it is imperative to establish a balance and let students understand how to self-evolve and gradually implement new views and perspectives. Students have to be cleverly coerced into the drive for a future-oriented mindset, and not fear punishment by the corporate world. Which brings us to the fact that too many programs foster risk-averse attitudes in the participants.

One of the criticisms mentioned earlier pertained to the need for business program participants to develop a conceptual reading and cohesive mindset about management, providing participants with wide powers of strategic analysis based on working with principles as opposed to practices.

Reflection makes individuals think about managerial practices and develop an epistemology of inquiry that allows them to contribute to the knowledge base by better asking the pertinent questions. A deeper understanding of reflective practices is also important to free managers from habitual and rigid ways of looking at phenomena, and to increase their alertness, creativity and innovation. In business education, however, insufficient attention has been given to "reflective management," and to steering the theory of practice and a deeper understanding of reflective practices. As a consequence, graduates are not good at developing a vision, nor in articulating and communicating that vision. Instead, they have a short-term rather than a long-term horizon.

Besides, insufficient attention is given to processes. Working in teams is one thing, but understanding team processes, group dynamics, giving and receiving feedback, and coaching is another thing. Generally, a common complaint is that the development of behavioral skills has no priority in business education. Personal development and personality development are elements most schools don't particularly focus on. It is assumed that through the pressures of an MBA-type program or the intensity of management development seminars that these competencies and elements will be developed. This is a "drifting" learning theory, not "steering" directly to the important points, which leaves a very high margin for error, i.e., students not understanding the importance of personal development, as well as not being able to develop others. The lack of personal and personality development is also illustrated by the way students are assessed. The role of assessment should not only include academic but also managerial and organizational components as well as incorporating a broader strategic perspective focusing on the student's recognition and understanding of the complexities and turbulence of today's and tomorrow's business, organizational and managerial environments. Moreover, business education must transfer a philosophy of management development as a continuing process of advancement and learning-to-learn.

It has been said that most business programs emphasize social capital (networking) under the umbrella of intellectual capital (knowledge) while completely ignoring cultural capital. Indeed, few institutions embrace the development of a mature view on geopolitics and socioeconomic trends. But even fewer attempt to increase the overall cultural level of their customers, such as to develop aesthetics, the art of living, or an appreciation of philosophical and cultural differences, which actually give meaning to the world in which they work - the medium where senses and wisdom meet each other.

An important number of educators and program coordinators will claim to have answered the criticisms the business community has identified. Indeed, we can find programs that have incorporated some elements of these criticisms, or we can find programs specifically aimed at reacting to these criticisms. Some institutions have responded by starting singular courses or seminars, others have initiated a personal development track, and still others have tried integrative modules or "learning-by-doing" projects (i.e. action learning). An interesting point still remains though, which is that the business community has emphasized its disappointment in the same areas of all types of business programs for at least the past twenty years. As a consequence, we must reflect upon whether the pedagogical models or approaches have actually fundamentally changed, or if there is indeed still a lot of critical work to do.

2.   PEDAGOGICAL METAPHORS

Pedagogical metaphors are used to describe the existing paradigms or approaches of a school, and the role of its different players. A look at these metaphors will better depict the essence of some of the criticisms described earlier. We'll synchronically present some of the established metaphors. Over the years, the transfer metaphor has been the prevailing one.

The transfer metaphor shows an approach to education as a theory of knowledge or subject matter that is considered as a transferable commodity. The student is viewed as a (passive) vessel positioned alongside a loading dock while the teacher is a crane or a forklift. The teacher delivers and places knowledge into the empty vessel until it is full. Once the vessel is filled, a "bill of lading," which is the diploma, certifies the content of the vessel. Monitoring a student means monitoring the process of filling the vessel and sometimes sampling the quality of the contents. When students fail, teachers will say that the vessel is no good. At the same time, the student will blame the forklift. It is clear that programs which are based on the transfer theory are very much lecture-based, including lectures from leading figures in their relevant fields (the more the better), providing students with duplicated course notes. The "in search of excellence" literature started by Peter and Waterman perfectly illustrates this approach. Conceptual routines are complemented by dynamic examples and prescriptions derived from the exploits of corporate heroes and "excellent" companies. Combined with the professional orientation to management, this type of approach, and the one discussed in the next paragraph, still prevails in most business schools.

The next metaphor is referred to as the shaping theory. In this metaphor, the student enters school as a piece of inert raw material, like a piece of wood or metal. The teacher is the craftsman who is able to give shape to the wood or metal, using subject matters as tools. Teaching methods that apply to the shaping theory include workshops, practical instructions similar to recipes and exercises with predictable outcomes. Again, students are seen implicitly as passive learners in the sense that they cannot take charge of their own learning and that they cannot use conceptual knowledge unless re-interpreted for them and delivered using carefully reconstructed methods. Instructors go to great length to ensure a well-presented and fine-tuned delivery, and to make sessions active and practical using nicely sequenced hands-on activities, cases, and exercises. As a consequence, the monitoring process focuses on the size and shape of the wood or the metal as it is being worked. If it all goes wrong, the student will blame the teacher for being a bad craftsman (i.e. bad delivery), whereas the teacher will say that the raw material is of poor quality. Some of the educational reforms are based on this shaping theory. The shaping theory, in conjunction with the transfer theory, accounts for most business school curricula today.

The travelling metaphor takes quite a different approach. The teacher takes the role of the experienced and expert guide who initiates and guides the students through an unknown terrain that s/he needs to explore. The guide not only points out the way, but also provides navigation tools and techniques: maps and compasses. The most common 'teaching methods' (if one can still call them such) under a travelling metaphor approach are more experiential-oriented: simulations, projects, action-learning exercises with unpredictable outcomes, discussions and independent learning. Action-learning emphasizes learning-by-doing. It is based on the idea that students learn more effectively with and from managers and teachers while all are engaged in the solution of actual, real-time and real-life problems occurring in a work-setting, applying the normal business pressures and constraints of organizational realities to ensure a high quality outcome. In programs that embrace this theory, monitoring means regularly comparing each other's travelling notes. Instructors blame student's failure on the unwillingness to take risks, be creative, or failing to accomplish objectives. From the student's point of view, the teacher can be blamed for poor guidance, poor equipment and imposing too many restrictions. Indeed, teachers that work within this approach not only need to master specialized skills, equipment and expertise, but also have to possess a good knowledge of the "terrain." Also, organizational sponsors can hamper the process by sanctioning projects and therefore active learning. Experiments have shown that this theory is particularly effective in masters-level education.

The growing theory takes us one step further. In many respects, this metaphor does not differ greatly from the previous one. It is rather an extension of the travelling metaphor that focuses more on student self-initiative. Rather than creating a body of knowledge, which would define the profession of management like the professional approach would take, subject matter is seen as a set of experiences each student should absorb. Hence, the overall aim for the student is also to focus on his/her personality. The student is pictured as a garden in which everything is already planted, but which still needs to grow. But grass doesn't grow by pulling it. The teacher's role is more that of a gardener, but he must be careful not to overwork the garden. Achieving a nice, full green garden of grass takes work and nurturing, but too much water or too much cutting will also result in a negative outcome. Hence, the gardener has to work that delicate balance by providing enabling constraints yet ensuring guidance. The methods used by a gardener are very much the same as those used when applying the travelling theory, only they allow the student even more freedom and room to experiment. Besides, the teacher is not the repository of what needs to be known and learned. As it is assumed that becoming a manager, in many respects, is working on one's own personality, the monitoring process consists of monitoring the personal development of the student. The student's commitment and realistic expectations in combination with a tutor who is competent in coaching personal development provides the ideal learning situation.

3.   CHALLENGES FOR EDUCATIONAL PRINCIPLES

We have discussed some consequences of the rapid, discontinuous, and nonlinear changes of today's economy, their quantitative and qualitative leaps (flux), the technological revolution, the collapse of time and space, and the increase of complexity affecting so many aspects of corporate and managerial life. Another important issue concerns the challenges for education. If the new task is to educate and develop students for highly dispersed, flexible, unstable organizations, with great emphasis on value-reinventing processes, the educational community must increasingly address issues of identifying, understanding and articulating information, experience and knowledge. Hence, the learning environment should more be considered as a place where students and teachers can find and examine their "voices" and their reading, understanding, and insights in an integrated way.

The major educational challenge could be described as bringing theory together with practice instead of a separated development of theory and practice. As has already become clear in discussing criticisms, the essence of theory lies in providing students with a framework in which they are able to translate a phenomenon to a conceptual level, come to an understanding by asking pertinent questions, and translating that understanding back to a practical level. The practice offered in a traditional program, however, is seen as a supplement to lectures - practical elements yet sheltered from daily practice. This constitutes a first challenge, namely how to approach theory and practice together?

Further, as we explained, management education is traditionally and substantially designed around different disciplines (marketing, finance, ...) with separate theories, different conceptual bases, and practical examples that presume to reflect the separate disciplines in the field of management. This phenomenon is also known as compartmentalization. Focusing on input and on developing the right courses in the right disciplines, the different component parts are then taught separately to students. To reiterate, bringing theory together with practice constitutes a major challenge for teaching and curriculum today.

3.1.   On Theory and Practice

Let's ask ourselves what theory and practice are all about? Theories can be situated on the cross-line between epistemology and a philosophical psyche. They are networks of intelligibility, knowledge, experience and meanings occurring within a turbulent environment. It is important, however, to look further than the content of knowledge and treating it as a simple informational commodity, and to focus on the dynamic process as well. Hence, the educational community should be interested in the potential of theories to offer new possibilities. Theories give experience with a critical distance and cohesive mindset. In other words, what is needed is the opportunity to think about things as psychological events. Hence, educators should approach theories as reflection-in-action. This reflection-in-action gives rise to the development of an epistemology of inquiry, which allows students to contribute to the knowledge base by better asking pertinent questions. Concerned with understanding the origin, nature and validity of knowledge, or the theory of (in this case) inquiry, reflection-in-action includes an epistemology of practice. Hence, theory and practice become inseparable. In other words, the business simulations, personal journals, peer reviews, specific team building and leadership modules, multidisciplinary case studies, and computer simulations that are used to make business education more pragmatic, are not the answer. An epistemology of inquiry based on working with best principles will enable people to search limitations from a critical distance. It will offer an integrative insight and an ability to translate managerial practice to a conceptual level, come to an understanding, and translate that understanding back to a practical level. Hence, the answer lies much more in an overall teaching philosophy in which the art of inquiry is central.

3.2.   Teaching in a Learning Community

Teaching, as Lundberg suggested, becomes less a "set of problems to be solved" and more "a set of dilemmas to live with." New ways of understanding and managing the anxiety and confusion associated with complexity, paradoxical roles, perpetual novelty, identities and meanings that arise here-and-now are needed. Answers to problems become problems about answers. Knowledge and information focus on the way one learns to fix the flow of the world in temporal and spatial terms and gives order to managerial complexity and chaos. This can be reflected in the learning environment by valuing diversities of perspectives and opinions. Examining competing frames of reference suggests a plurality of discourses and mindsets instead of reducing student's perception to a single all-inclusive grand "master" theory. As described earlier, theories offer the opportunity to think about things as psychological events. Valuing diversities of perspectives, areas and disciplines around a particular issue while identifying the underlying principles and uncovering structuring processes, gives rise to a higher potential of knowledge to process. Diversity also makes clear that knowledge itself becomes a matter of governance.

In transferring knowledge, teachers are invited to act as mentors, and facilitators who make tacit knowledge more explicit, within a subtle mixture of coaching, negotiated authority and learned freedom. In this process, the teacher sometimes takes responsibility for learning, while sometimes this responsibility is shifted to students. Students work with their mentors and learn by observation and practice. The close relationship and alliance between them can be seen as a subtle mixture of education and knowledge creation, of dialoguing to create shared meanings, of ethics and aesthetics. Knowledge sometimes has to be repackaged for students and delivered by carefully reconstructed methods and substantial debriefing. As such, coaching and learned freedom give a sense of experience that can be further developed and applied. It is in this way that an epistemology of inquiry can be developed. Hence, the educational setting should be configured as a collaborative forum, a learning community in which different stakeholders (program heads, faculty, executives, advisory boards, corporate action-learning sponsors) and students mutually engage in developing new understandings, approaches and unbounded sets of perspectives. Within this learning community, stakeholders participate as partners in a mutual undertaking to advance learning and thereby shape educational provision. The learning community is a vehicle for sharing experiences, information, ideas, and knowledge. Members of this community will also find the moral and emotional support for learning. In other words, this learning community could be considered a learning organization.

Active participation is to be regarded as an opportunity to interpret the world from the student's point of view and frame of understanding. By offering students a platform of free dialogue, individuals are confronted with challenges that are paradoxical and which cannot once and for all be defined or resolved. At the same time it is important to emphasize the role of the learning community, which is a platform for individuality, participation, and differentiation, structuring the open learning environment, in which diverse working and content forms, perspectives, and issues take place simultaneously, becomes one of the major challenges.

It is clear that experience and knowledge creation are not based on simple information processing as students are not simply passive recipients of expertise but rather co-creators of their here-and-now learning. Learning is characterized more by interpretation than by description and analysis. It is a journey through the world in which individuals live, and through networks of self-knowledge and self-development. This self-knowledge should include elements such as preferred learning style(s).

3.3.   An Integrated Curriculum

We want to take the discussion one step further now: from teaching philosophy to program philosophy, that is the curriculum. As we mentioned before, business schools and management institutes have been altering the design of their programs in response to several of the criticisms pertaining to the model of business education. This model is based on technical proficiency similar to that required to solve straightforward problems in mathematics, physics, or engineering. The left curve in figure 3-1 shows how this functional and compartmentalized approach has been reflected in business programs since the 1970s. One can question whether the business curriculum has truly and fundamentally changed since then.

Essentially, changes have included more integrative clusters that weave together common themes from multiple and multidisciplinary angles, action learning based consulting projects, or personal development tracks. These can be found in most management education programs since the second half of the 1980s or in most cases since the 1990s. This is shown in the right curve of figure 3-1.

Many institutions use a mixture of both approaches: starting with some functional courses, programs then focus on more integrative modules. Another alternative that is often presented, uses integrative modules to conclude every semester or block of functional courses. This method should help students to have a more integrated insight, and gives a better understanding of how the different classes relate to a unified whole program. Although in most cases the student is still considered a more passive learner, aspects of the travelling metaphor can be found in programs when also combined with a more experiential approach.

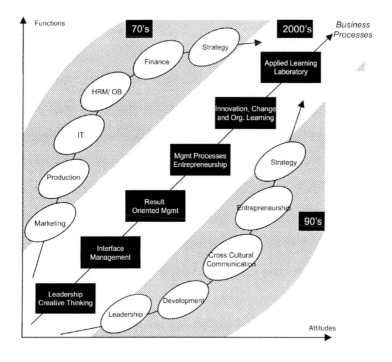

Figure 3-1. The integrated curriculum

Some institutions take it a step further and offer programs that have a common theme. We don't hereby mean the "major" of some MBA programs offered, but rather a complete MBA program with a common theme like technology, or luxury brand management, among others. Also in corporate (executive) education, only few programs really have a well-defined theme that underlies and streamlines the whole program. This means more than just putting on a title, but a theme that really reflects the philosophy and design of that particular program.

Others offer completely problem-based or issue-based programs. Managerial roles, however, seldom rely on just solving problems - straightforward or not. Besides, problems are not the key in managerial roles, since not everything is a problem. Again, in this we see the technocratic or professional approach that starts from the assumption that through problem-finding and problem-solving, stability, coordination, integration, and the implementation of functionality are pursued.

The Economist's Intelligence Unit, in a recent report, stated that the key factors for driving an organization's competitive advantage lie in a focus on business processes. This is consistent with the newer management paradigms that have increasingly concentrated on business, organizational and strategic processes as a way to discuss value creation. Besides, the new economic realities and their complexities as described in the beginning of this book illustrate the importance of understanding processes.

We are convinced that the future of the "business school" will entail curricula focusing on business processes, progressing towards the use of a learning laboratory. The third arrow in figure 3-1 shows this perspective. Mental models are also central to the design of learning laboratories. Laboratories are mental model practice fields, where people develop the skills to have a dialogue about their assumptions in "real time" - in the moment they are dealing with an issue. This practice field enables people to talk coherently about beliefs and attitudes, to hear comments about them, to question them, and to look more clearly at sources and opportunities.

4. EXPERIENCES WITH EDUCATIONAL TECHNOLOGIES IN MANAGEMENT DEVELOPMENT: LESSONS FOR THE FUTURE

For companies, the surge in management development initiatives and executive education is not only about gaining an edge in the market. Along with a vibrant economy, companies are using management education as a tool to foster or win back the loyalty of staff, recapturing lost talents, or as a lure for new hires. Recent mergers, joint ventures and alliances have enhanced the role of corporate education and corporate universities. Along with the rising demand, however, has come rising standards. Flexibility, more customized and real-time programs, and time efficiency both inside and outside the office are some of the new main focal points. In the next section, we are going to see how these demands are translated in the rise of new educational technologies. What lessons can we learn from different players in the educational arena?

4.1. Open Learning Experiences

The academic institutes created in order to experiment with open or distance learning are in most countries the so-called Open Universities (OU). Open Universities fit the movement in the 1960s and 1070s towards lower entry requirements for university studies. Furthermore, authors and philosophers like Ivan Illich, advocated the need for continuous, lifelong learning. Open universities were not created to cater the same target groups as regular universities but rather to the "convenience" and second chance markets. OUs therefore developed a greater experience with more flexible forms of management education. Because they have experience in creating a more "open learning" environment such as distance learning, OUs offer the closest to what is called a "virtual" approach to education. As such, Open Universities are now becoming part of the "virtualization race."

Virtual business school is commonly understood as the use of information technology, and increasingly network technology to replace the classical educational model of classroom instruction. Students receive material in electronic form, via the Internet or on CD ROMs, and they use networks in order to communicate with their tutors. Some forms of virtual education use a synchronous mode: the two ends (teacher and student) are connected at the same time and can communicate with each other, such as with video conferencing. Other forms use the asynchronous mode, where the student can use the network for various reasons such as to mail things, but does not get two-way online communication. Most web-based teaching is asynchronous. What is commonly known today as virtual education is an ICT based replacement of the pedagogical transfer mode, used in classical classroom teaching.

The transfer paradigm, however "open," flexible and catering to the specific situation of the customer, still prevails within the OU environment. Generally speaking, the approach is rather traditional. Students are given paper-based and electronic material, and they can have contact with tutors through regional centers or a main campus. The material generally focuses on questions of reflection and activities for individual students to do. These activities, however, don't necessarily develop management skills. Group activities are limited or nonexisting, and there's not a great deal of project-based work. And, in the end, assuming that knowledge can be transferred and measured, exams will decide who awarded a degree. Particularly in the case of management education for practicing managers, the measurement of knowledge as a single measure for learning is, as argued before, questionable.

The flexibility offered by OUs is shown through the distance learning mode as well as the lack of time constraints. Every student can work through the material at his or her own pace and time availability. Little or no flexibility is offered, however, within the different courses or in the different degree programs. It should be recognized, though, that distance learning material created and developed by OUs can generally be of good educational quality and design.

The need for continuous and flexible learning has increased, and as distance learning has been deemed to be a lucrative business, several classical universities have jumped on the bandwagon. For example, Europe's Henley Management School has entered the OU market by offering flexible distance learning programs and by establishing small campuses throughout Europe and the Commonwealth. The University of Liverpool (UK) successfully launched a fully ICT-based distance learning MBA. They created a venture (under franchise) outside the university with a different brand (KIT label). This construction allows more degrees of freedom compared to a more regulated university setting. In few years time, they have developed a annual student intake of thousands, from around the world. The US-based University of Phoenix was a pioneer in distance learning and now boasts thousands of degree students, using a mixture of online electronic and paper-based delivery. Audio, videotapes, and videoconferencing are other technologies used in distance education.

Duke university's Fuqua School of Business is a pioneer in offering a first-class electronic MBA program by using a platform of leading-edge applications. Students use CD-ROM video lectures in which the professor appears to be actively teaching onscreen and they have supplemental video and audio programs which can be downloaded. Further, students work with peers via bulletin boards, E-mail and live online chats. Last, face-to-face contact with faculty and other students has not disappeared. Some two-week mandatory modules for onsite classes and meetings with business owners across Europe, China, South America and the United States are part of the program.

Over the last decade, we have seen a rapid move of many classical universities, including the top US programs like Stanford and MIT, into the same market of open learning based on IT. Those universities have concentrated most of their effort on regular students, rather than on the second chance student of open universities. The vast number of universities offering online education today proves the growing interest of the use of ICT in management education.

The same top universities, like MIT, decided recently to make their pedagogical material (the material of the faculty) available to the outside world at no cost. Though this has nothing to do with the pedagogical delivery and/or diploma offering, it is an exciting new development in the area of ICT-based learning. It shows is a changing mindset concerning virtual learning platforms, even among those already established. On the other hand, it only confirms the prevailing transfer metaphor.

Despite the large offering of open learning from classical universities into this segment, as well as the acquired experience, the paradigm of the educational process has not yet changed. Open learning is still based on the transfer paradigm, in which ICT is considered to be the crane that loads the empty ship in a faster way. The more classical universities enter into the market of open learning, the more focus on content and 'brand' of a degree. The OUs, at least, focused on the pedagogical side of the educational process from the start.

Conferences about online education focus on the experiences of open learning in both Open Universities and classical universities offering open learning. We can we look at different experiences in an open learning environment, both from the point of view of OUs and regular universities. We should investigate what lessons could be learned and applied to future developments.

We shall commence with the experience of OUs, as they have made a major contribution to the existing knowledge of ICT and education. Open Universities will be defined as a kind of mega-university with a student population of over 100,000. OUs are growing rapidly with the ever-increasing need for worldwide education, particularly in the third world. As the volume of potential students increases, ICT based distance education becomes a more efficient and less expensive way to learn. Broadband PC connections, however, are not yet widely available, so large scale technological usage in OUs cannot be implemented. As a consequence, these mega-universities use the same technology and methods as classical universities. Open Universities, for example, use a great deal of audio and videotapes, and (public) broadcasting.

The British OU is a good example of this approach. Today, these universities experiment with 'personal casting' which entails transmitting programs via the Internet onto the PC of the student. It remains, though, a one-way transfer. Open universities experiment as well with remote classrooms, particularly in countries like Australia, where distance is the main reason for the success of open learning.

Increasingly, those running OUs are discovering the "knowledge media" that supports the conversational paradigms and community ideas. But particularly within this evolution towards knowledge media, the mass of students they cater to becomes a burden for them in the ICT development they would like to undertake. Students experiment with e-mail, asynchronous computer conferencing (compared with chatting over the Internet), Internet/ worldwideweb and stand-alone multimedia, but due to the large numbers of students, the interaction remains limited. We can learn from OUs that ICT is indeed able to improve the value of learning, but ICT is not able to cater to large numbers.

OUs do give attention to the changing role of the faculty. Not only do they continue to use tutors as a first line support for students, but they also train them in electronic mediation. Some of the OUs, in particular the British OU, have developed a high level expertise in electronic mediation techniques and training for tutors using them. The enormous numbers of students, however, make it extremely difficult to apply electronic mediation. Despite the remarkable expertise they possess in electronic mediation, the pedagogical metaphor supporting their education does not allow effective use of it.

In regular universities, web-based teaching is often used in experiments with open learning. Course material is offered over the Internet, as well as via electronic conferencing (mostly asynchronous) and tutors support students via e-mail. Students can create their own agenda. There's also an attempt to foster electronic teamwork among students, but with varying success. Regular universities successfully use multimedia to make case-studies more attractive (including video), and for language learning.

There are also lessons to be learned from regular university's experiences in open learning. Recent conferences like the IFIP conference on virtual education and the Educa On-Line Conference, highlighted a few interesting points, which we will now discuss.

The first challenge is the need for accreditation, and in general, more credibility for open learning degrees. Traditionally, a university's credibility stems from its physical existence and its knowledge resources, including faculty and the tradition of the university. ICT-based approaches basically lack these physical assets, causing confusion first about credibility, and very certainly if obtaining a degree remains the main purpose of academic education. It is fair to say that among academics and academic culture, open learning is not considered to be the highest standard of education. As we will point out later in this chapter, this lack of credibility may be one of the reasons why corporate (virtual) universities have become more popular. The accreditation and credibility within a corporate environment is given by the employer to the employee, which is at least clear and direct, and with concise purpose and consequences.

A second challenge of creating success of ICT-based open learning approaches is the need for digital libraries, which allow a purely web-based approach to succeed. The web-based teaching approach offers a wide range of hard-to-find resources via the Internet, but it generally lacks books and journal articles, important resources for learning. The recent initiatives of, for example, MIT offering their material for free might change that in the future. However, we will have to see in what format the material will be made available, and how easy it will be to create a real electronic library starting from the base material.

As we previously stated briefly, companies are increasingly entering the market of flexible learning. The corporate presence in flexible learning has evoked some interesting debate concerning the open learning offerings of classical universities. The web is central to most corporate and academic educational experiments. Often, companies start by offering some part of the educational process themselves, but, companies organize the learning process differently than universities. Corporate learning tends to be learner-centered, but relatively weak in the content part of the courses. Universities, however, remain organized in functional areas, so courses offered by open learning in universities follow this functional subdivision. The knowledge content of each individual course is therefore stronger, but the overall programs often lack integration and a clear focus on managerial competencies. Within a corporate setting, education is much more skill-based and problem/ solution oriented.

There are other observations that can identified from these experiences. For example, the more ICT is used in education, the more intensive communication becomes, and therefore the smaller the group of students who work together should become in order to remain manageable. Also, we can question whether the transfer paradigm can be continued to be used when the aim is individualized management education of experienced people.

The experiments that both universities and companies are making raise a fundamental issue of whether we are witnessing a technological evolution or a fundamental paradigm shift. The observation that the introduction of IT-based education appears to be more difficult in existing university settings than in corporate settings, seems to suggest the latter. The fundamental paradigm shift we propose is that management education is more learner-centered, with the long term perspective being to offer individualized management education: just-in-time, just enough, and just right education.

Corporate virtual universities are rapidly becoming popular, and therefore we want to touch upon corporate experiences in management education. First we want to give some insight into experiences in corporate management development programs and secondly we want to relate that experience to the role of ICT in corporate management education.

4.2.   The Corporate Educational Environment

Although business schools and management institutes control the bulk of the management development market, some newer approaches are popping up in companies' in-house programs, corporate learning institutes or corporate universities. Potentially, the most appropriate corporate education allows for the development of the skills and competencies individuals lack and those which a particular company needs, to be incorporated into a company-wide organizational development project, in which the core values and culture of the learning organization can be established.

As management training is seen as a major influencer of key strategic success factors, with direct impact on a company's bottom line and maximizing business results, and more skills are now demanded of non-management employees, the number of companies in the US with a corporate university or learning center has consistently increased. In a Business Week report on executive education, it is professed that number has gone up from 400 to 1600 over the last decade. That number is still growing rapidly, a trend that is also catching on in Europe.

For large corporations that spend as much as $500,000 a year on training and education, a complete e-learning solution or service not only is more convenient than a patchwork of services, but may also result in potential cost savings such as travel costs or salary costs. The reason is that major e-learning companies build courses as well as host them, maintain them, and offer interactive tutoring, security mechanisms, and libraries of off-the-shelf programs (such as certification-training courses). They also provide quite detailed services like transforming paper-bound guides or tutorials into online training programs.

Some of the techniques used in these innovative programs are a clear (and sometimes complete) focus on the company's issues and bottom-line goals, action-learning inside projects, mentor programs, and self-teaching and learning through the group. Faculty from business schools and experts in the field act in these programs in a variety of roles: internal consultants, teachers, project supervisors, program designers, liaisons between the company and the providers, and program coordinators. Together with faculty, company leaders and speakers run sessions and real-life business cases. This trend not only enhances content and delivery, but many companies find it offers a better fit with career development and an overall training path or development strategy, strategic change, and organizational growth processes. There's also the plus of lower cost. Specific modules from one program, for example, can be re-designed and used in another training and development path. Last, it offers more flexibility. As there's no single business school that is strong in every field of expertise, it enables companies to look for the individual professors and experts that fit the company's needs or industry, and work directly with them. We can now understand why some of the more innovative programs are found not in business schools, but rather within the corporate institute environment.

Virtual learning requires an architecture that supports content, delivery, business strategy, governance issues, competency frameworks, technology, and customer needs. In 2002, companies who are leaders in training investments will spend over 30% of their training time on technology-based delivery mechanisms. This goes from rudimentary technologies like CD ROM to very sophisticated learning portals. Virtual learning portals rarely provide, however, a mechanism to manage all courses and learning initiatives that a company needs as well as learning events that take place with customers, suppliers, and partners. They often fail to regulate employee access, analyze learning effectiveness, and track budgets. Several technology players try to fill this particular gap. Cisco's Networking Management System, for example, is an e-learning model that delivers web-based content, online testing, and performance tracking as well as quality assurance.

4.2.1. The Case of a Corporate MBA

One innovative example can be drawn from the European headquarters of a high-tech multinational that developed plans for its own European corporate MBA program, based on a consortium model. The company had been confronted with strong competition, changing technologies, changing customer demands and changing market segments. The less loyal customer had demanded more sophisticated and reliable products, and better service. As a consequence, the company built a new vision for the future, taking into account the changing markets and business infrastructures. The new competitive agenda entailed new goals and objectives based on the development of core competencies and an increase in needed capabilities, an improvement in the processes of innovation, knowledge, entrepreneurship, and creativity. The project commenced with an assessment of the human capital of the firm as well as their needs for the future. This assessment was the basis for the general management development plan and cultural change linked to individual development. The purpose of individual development was insight in the flux and process of knowledge as well as a broader base of knowledge to apply when faced with business challenges and complexities, and to create a learning-to-learn culture. The purpose was to increase the participant's role as strategic partners and change agents within the organization.

The decision making process to commence a corporate MBA was very long. A variety of initiatives and possibilities were discussed. One possibility was made up of modules which were part of a horizontal (different topics, same level) as well as a vertical (increasing complexity within the same topic) development path. The added value of each alternative was assessed in relation to the overall corporate strategy and vision. Eventually, the company decided to embark on a corporate MBA program, as part of an overall management development (or Human Resources Development - HRD) initiative because the program would bring the needed level of competencies, knowledge, and learning strategies that were identified in the assessment. Particular modules from the MBA program could also be simplified and used in other development paths. In other words, they would "cascade" into other either more basic or more specialized development programs. The company viewed this cascading to be an economic as well as strategic move, as they would count on faster development in the future, and a multiple implementation of the modules at a reduced costs.

The philosophy or purpose behind this program can be described as: the merger between management concepts with company-specific organizational and business themes; the creation of new behavior and a knowledge-generating culture; an evolution from routine to creativity; and entrepreneurship linked to the overall company vision. Management competencies were used as a basis for the design of the program. By merging functional areas with behavioral areas, the creators of the program envisioned a generalist approach to management.

In our example, the company appointed an independent program coordinator who ran the program as an interim manager. The coordinator's role was the main designer, developer, and organizer of the program. He also played an important liaison role, that between the company and the educational providers (business schools and individual instructors from management institutes and the company), and between the participants, the HR Department and management. He was also actively involved in the selection of the providers and of the participants. Once the program started, he briefed instructors about the company and the program's philosophy, assessed content and materials, and ensured, through coaching, the participants' personal development.

The program was carefully designed to meet the company's objectives and key concepts, while still maintaining an 80-20 balance between generic management concepts and specific critical issues. First a number of concepts and techniques were introduced and then they were used to further discuss relevant issues and challenges for the company. At the same time this approach created a balance between the strategic and the operational levels within companies. On a conceptual level, new and innovative models and concepts were used. This had an important impact on the selection of faculty and business institutes that would be involved in the program. Furthermore, the program was designed to increase the complexity of the issues, and therefore the discussion, throughout the program. As a direct consequence of the specific company context and needs, the program was developed with a European theme and strong strategic and marketing components. The European theme was reflected in every course. In addition, a specific European module was incorporated into the program. It covered the role and function of European institutes and the European Commission, as well as an introduction into European legislation, with a special emphasis on competition law.

The 15-month program consisted of close to two-thirds of a regular MBA program. The idea behind the consortium model - several affiliate organizations and several management institutes - was to combine the company affiliate's home-countries (regional organizations) with a Pan-European view, mixed with different business education methods, approaches and expertise of several management institutes. The creators of the program envisioned a true exchange of cross-cultural and cross-business experiences. An additional advantage was that no particular management institute was "dominating" the program so that the company was not solely associated and "dependent" on the quality of one single management institute. Quality (content and logistics), location, facilities, and expertise in a particular field were key in the choice of the participating management institutions.

After the positive decision by the company to start a "company MBA," the coordinator developed a communication strategy to inform and motivate staff to join the program. At the same time, the company defined selection criteria similar to the typical MBA requirements, coupled with some additional company-specific criteria. Throughout the selection procedure, candidates' supervisors were coached to ensure their active support in their role as mentor.

A kick-off weekend was organized two weeks prior to the "official" start of the program. The weekend was used as an important introductory phase for the participants. The coordinators explained the content and organization of the program and held a discussion about participants' expectations and the expectations of management. They were also thrown into a business simulation game to expose them on thinking about the dynamics among different functionalities within a given organization. Group development, self-assessment and development were the central focus, as well as the coaching role of the program coordinators. Participants also completed a management competency test, which gave a competency profile of themselves. They were given personal feedback by a person certified for this specific test and, after peer discussions and self-reflection, they had to develop a personal development (learning) plan aimed at increasing certain competencies which were closely linked to their individual career development, personal agendas and career activities.

The MBA program was designed to avoid altogether any on-the-job disturbances, so as not to affect their performance nor to upset any of their managers and supervisors. Therefore, the first part of the program was based heavily on the use of technology, particularly electronic data transfer and print materials. As such, the program designer incorporated a heavy distance education base into the program. The distance education feature also included distance teaching, the instructor's role in the process, and distance learning, the student's role in the process. Especially in the first part of the program - the basic courses - they used straight distance learning: a combination of electronic instruction together with paper based learning (paper and pencil), introducing mini-cases and additional reading to the students, and live and videotaped programming, augmented by textbooks, handbooks, computer programs, multimedia and other instructional materials (CD-ROM, simulations, etc.). Individual tutoring was available where needed. Also, students could exchange information and experiences via the

Internet, or search for information through Internet sources. One-way interaction, standard presentation of materials to all students, standard, structured practice, and instant, specific feedback and feed-forward were combined with learning at one's individual pace and according to one's own time schedule.

The second part of the program followed what would be considered a more traditional "sit-in" formula. Intensive one-week blocks took place in the partnering management institutes once every six weeks. In between two modules, participants had to complete assignments and prepare the forthcoming module. The blocks were issue-based, multidisciplinary, and integrative. Self-assessment, peer-learning, project work and case building became an integral part of the learning tools. Throughout the program, faculty from different disciplines acted as facilitators, coaches and mirrors to the students.

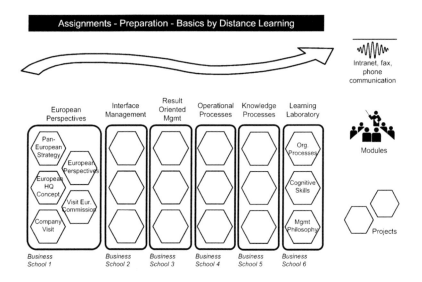

Figure 3-2. Model of a corporate MBA

The group was in need of an injection of energy and motivation after about the six-month mark, so a post-summer-break outdoor weekend was organized. The weekend focused on leadership and teambuilding exercises through the element of adventure, briefing and debriefing sessions, coaching and camaraderie. It was not so much the "adventure" element which was in the end so important, rather the application of conceptual thoughts and ideas to practical challenges, individual and group (practices, principles and conceptual) feedback, and professional coaching. The important role of the program coordinator again was quite evident in the coaching role of this energy-rejuvenating weekend.

The final piece of the overall program puzzle was an action-learning graduating project, in which the participants acted as internal consultants working on real-life issues. These projects were vital to the overall "education" of the participants, as they made participants integrate conceptual knowledge with practical company experience, individual learning with team learning, and gather hands-on project management experience. These projects entailed real (i.e. already pending in the company) business development and strategic issues. This forced participants to identify academic and theoretical principles with which to implement solutions to managerial and business challenges. During the two to three month projects, participants worked under the supervision of both an academic and a company advisor as well, to gently "guide" students when they may have veered slightly into the wrong direction. The company also considered the projects as an important element of the return-on-investment, as they could see a highly visible, tangible and substantial contribution to overall organizational development at a relatively low cost (compared to similar projects done by an outside consulting firm). Also the project's implementation became much more likely in light of the fact that there were several stakeholders of that project within the organization both during and after the project.

4.2.2. Information Technologies

The understanding of corporate universities seems highly correlated with the evolution of the technological possibilities for ICT based education. Not only do companies create more and more corporate universities, but they almost exclusively base them on an ICT platform for knowledge and information sharing. They all seem to recognize the tremendous push that ICT can give to the corporate development activities. Nevertheless, most of them are aware of the necessity to have a correct vision on ICT for education, in order to use it successfully: a vision that is embedded in the overall corporate strategy.

Meister describes with a remarkable sense of detail some of the experiences on this subject, mainly made in the US. Those experiences provide us with some thoughtful insights in the reasons for failure or success in our own efforts, while we explain the building of the Hybrid Business School in the next chapters.

Technology is considered as an enabler to accelerate learning. Effective learning can only be obtained if the learning process is carefully tied to the strategic needs of the business. ICT based learning caters ideally to rather flat and flexible organizations. Successful experiments are often based on learning alliances, both within the company, as well as with outside partners of the company. Corporate universities often operate as a business and therefore follow the rules of commercial feedback.

Corporate universities are more a process than a place. Of course, certain aspects of the educational process, like face-to-face workshops and the university administration may need some physical buildings, but the education itself is linked to the process and not to the physical place. Corporate universities link learning paths to the personal development of employees, an interesting evolution pertaining to students' motivation and accreditation of learning. Employee self-development often linked to compensation, and career self-management is becoming a further motivator for learning. This approach proves to be successful.

Corporate universities are also piguing the interest of both clients and suppliers of a company. Sometimes, there's a creation of "communities-of-interest" around certain issues of common interest. Corporate universities equally fit the lifelong learning need of individual employees. In order to cater to different stakeholder interests, programs offered by corporate universities often contain the three following areas: core workplace competencies, corporate citizenship, and contextual issues.

A typical characteristic of an introduction of ICT in corporate universities is that it aims to create a continuous open learning laboratory available for the different stakeholders. Companies have a tendency to pay more attention to how technology transforms the learning process itself, compared to regular universities. Corporate virtual schools also pay a great deal of attention to an improved pedagogical approach, whereas the knowledge content of the courses seems of less immediate importance. Although these virtual learning laboratories use advanced technologies (like satellite classes, multimedia over the network, videoconferencing and web-based teaching), they don't get caught up in the ICT set up at the expense of the learning process itself. ICT-based learning in companies does pay attention to the learning process on which the courses are based. The drive for immediate applicability of learning seems to be a good motivator for corporate universities to explore the learning metaphors more in depth, rather than to experiment with more fancy technology as a gadget in itself. The economic drive, to be able to apply the acquired skills and knowledge immediately in the company could be the main distinction between successful and unsuccessful experiments in online learning.

Let us have a closer look at how companies go beyond the classical university and learning setting, with the aim of fostering learning and knowledge sharing. The innovative uses of new technologies such as the Internet suggest the close link between the effort of a company to develop knowledge management and the emerging success of newly created corporate (virtual) universities.

The emergence of the Internet and intranet technologies enabled a whole new range of possibilities. In the majority of its educational applications, however, the Internet is solely used as a powerful resource for structuring and navigating the information and communication spaces. People regularly describe communication technologies in conduit terms, talking of information as "in" books, files, or databases, information that can just as easily be accessed or "outsourced." We are asked to put ideas "down on paper," to "send them along," and so forth. As the example of Duke showed, the Internet can also be a powerful resource for constructing and negotiating the social space. Scattered groups of people and individuals, unknown to one another, even living in contiguous areas, and sometimes never seeing each other, are nonetheless able to form robust social worlds. In the professional environment this kind of self-created and self-organized groups are new, although, some companies already experiment with project based education using collaborative tools. A different appraisal of the working-learning-innovating triangle, however, supported by an informal ICT platform, can lead to the development of a process called "community-based knowledge refinement": an example of an emergent knowledge environment. Brown describes these organizations as communities-of-practice.

Communities-of-practice can have different forms. The first form is illustrated by the example of sales representatives. Sales representatives can form an online community of learning and sharing of experiences. If a sales representative has a particular problem at the client premises, and he cannot immediately find a solution, he can consult his network and discuss the issue with colleagues. Interesting problems and cases remain stored in the database for future consultation. Only the interesting and remarkable ones are stored. The same network or community is used for education and information sharing. Hansen and his colleagues describe a similar process of "personalization" as a tool used by consultants at firms such as Bain & Co. or McKinsey & Co. They focus on dialogue between individuals rather than (codified) knowledge objects in a database. Using networks of expertise and checking a "people finder" database, consultants can tap into a worldwide network of colleagues' experience. Knowledge is shared not only face-to-face but also by telephone, email, and video-conferences.

Another form of a community-of-practice is one which is created around a common area of interest, for example, diabetics. A community-of practice in this case could be created around a pharmaceutical company producing drugs for diabetics, a medical insurance company, medical staff and possibly the government. The common aim of the community-of-practice would be better and less expensive service for diabetics. This "inter-organizational" community could exchange information, conduct discussions, and give advice; a win-win situation for all. Above all, this community would create knowledge by its mere sharing of experiences.

With his concept of communities-of-practice, Brown attempts to give an integrated view on working, learning and innovating in a particular corporate situation. The complexity of contradictory forces that put an organization's assumptions and core beliefs in direct conflict with members' working, learning, and innovating arises from a thorough misunderstanding of the meaning of working, learning and innovating. The corporate tendency to down-skill can often lead to practice that is not described in rules and manuals, and to the creation of communities being driven further underground so that the insights gained through work are more completely hidden from the organization as a whole. Then later changes or reorganizations, whether or not intended to down-skill, may disrupt unnoticed practices. The gap between expected and actual practice may become too large to bridge. To close that gap, an organization will need to reconceive itself as a community-of-practice, acknowledging in the process the many unconventional or unauthorized communities in its midst.

Size of the company is not the single determining factor. Within an organization that is perceived as a collective of communities, and not simply that of individuals, and in which experimenting is acceptable, separate community perspectives can be communicated among groups. Out of this friction of competing ideas, improvisational sparks of organizational innovation can emerge. Sources of innovation can also lie outside an organization, among its customers and suppliers.

The organizational design and the paths in which communities are linked to one another could enhance the healthy autonomy of communities, while simultaneously building the interconnectedness through which the dissemination of separate communities' experiments occur. In some form or another the stories that support learning-in-working and innovation should be allowed to circulate. The technological potential to support this distribution (e-mail, bulletin boards and other devices that are capable of supporting narrative exchange) is available. Working-class groups (like the sales representatives) are remarkably open with one another and share knowledge. Within these communities, news travels fast and community knowledge is readily available to its members.

This view of communities-of-practice contrasts strongly with the perspective of the conventional workplace, where:
-   Work and learning are set out in formal descriptions so that people (and organizations) can be held accountable;
-   Groups are organized to define responsibility;
-   Organizations are bounded to enhance concepts of competition;
-   Peripheries are closed off to maintain secrecy and privacy.

While information technology has now become widely available and, particularly, the Internet has grown exponentially, the use of ICT has not significantly progressed. It is often simply reinforcing the classical metaphor of knowledge being poured by a teacher into an empty vessel (the student). Little attention has been given towards the reconceptualization of the traditional notions of teaching, instruction, the learner, the subject matter, the technology and the system, and transforming these into something quite different. Even if an instructor attempted to teach, it is not just justifiable to conclude that nothing was learned. The process is not, then, like the addition of a brick to a building, where the brick remains as distinct and self-contained as it was in the builder's hand. Instead, it is a little like the addition of color to color in a painting, where the color that is added becomes inseparably a part of the color that was there before. What is learned can never be judged solely in terms of what is taught.

Rabindranath Tagore once introduced an interesting metaphor of "stolen knowledge":

"A very great musician came and stayed in (our) house. He made one big mistake … (he) determined to teach me music, and consequently no learning took place. Nevertheless, I did casually pick up from him a certain amount of stolen knowledge".

Tagora "stole" knowledge by watching and listening to the musician as the latter, outside his classes, played for his own and others' entertainment. Part of the need to "steal" arises because relatively little of the complex web of actual practice can be made the subject of explicit instruction.

The work of Brown unfolds a rich and complex picture of what a situated view of learning needs to account for, and emphasizes in particular the social, rather than merely physical nature of "situatedness." Legitimate peripheral participation (LPP), which is Brown's understanding of learning, clearly distinguishes between learning and intentional instruction. The richness of interpersonal interaction is usually either overlooked or deliberately disrupted in the classroom. In the workplace, learners can, when they need, steal their knowledge from the social periphery, made up of other, more experienced workers and ongoing, socially shared practice. The classroom, unfortunately, tends to be too well secured against theft. Information technology should not reinforce the limitations of the classrooms, but rather allow for participative learning.

The particular example that Brown uses, is the one of 'Community-Based Knowledge Refinement' at Xerox. Web technology (http + html) made the network-of-networks, the Internet, accessible for a wider population. Within the view that innovation is in itself a joint activity of a number of "Complex Adaptive Systems" (CAS), Internet and the web can provide a medium for innovation.

Technology companies do not focus on products anymore, but on product platforms. These designed product platforms also tap into the company's tacit knowledge. Each product platform can put a number of product variants on the market. Furthermore, platforms themselves evolve through discontinuous changes in technology components, like the chromosome in the human being. All companies have in their "peripheries," but very often we do not see them and therefore we cannot learn from them.

As Brown's research with sales representatives at Xerox shows, an important, non-documented copy quality fault will be dealt with via "story-telling." Since telling stories seems to be how people learn, then the task for information technology is to create a "learning space" which allows self-learning via exchange of stories. In ICT terminology one would think about collaborative software.

Within Xerox, a process called Community-Based Knowledge Refinement has been put in place, by which representatives produce some cases (stories) that are put up to a peer review process. Referees appointed by the community then referee the retained cases before they are integrated in the Case Base. This mechanism leverages both social and technical learning. It is a social way to create and award good ideas. Particularly in technology driven industries, the award winning aspects prove to be motivating.

This case base is of immediate interest and use of to representatives, but it also allows further learning using learning algorithms. Genetic algorithms (based on sources of variability) are used to create a "community mind." Learning and adaptation, also in the "community mind," takes place through critique, cross coupling and combining "tips." With this approach, a vast space boils down to "knowledge."

The important questions for a company are how to facilitate this process, and how to foster its emergence. In leveraging the small efforts of many (people) so as to drive learning and innovation, web technology can be especially useful. However, web technology needs to be specifically organized in a way to facilitate this learning, and organizations seldom do this. Fortunately, "emergent practice" can be identified through "authorized practice." It is only a different subset.

A comparable example is the one of the medical insurance company, and the pharmaceutical company, together mediating a focus group for clients suffering from diabetes. This discussion forum is a self-organized group of people sharing the same interest, but facilitated by people from both companies. The companies provide the clients with information about how to improve their quality of life and well-being. Clients are happier because they are more informed and better served. The insurance company lowers its long-term expenses for diabetic clients and the pharmaceutical company gains direct access to its ultimate client. Hence, and in general, companies should attempt to identify the "emergent" much faster, a practice that contributes to core competencies, and as a whole, makes the company become a powerful entity pushing innovation. It reflects the capacity of creating new businesses, core products, end products and services through the mutation of capabilities and recombinations of resources rather than just fixing a few core competencies.

A possible and interesting way to support the emergent or "the social fabric" throughout companies is the use of hypertext technology within the framework of a "knowledge refinement server." In the case of Xerox, the knowledge refinement server allows people to contribute, as well as to reflect and learn from experiences and from each other. The advantage of hypertext links is that they enable building on existing thoughts, give comments, suggest new possibilities, and so on, comparable to the "story telling" approach described earlier. Linking comments, cross-linking comments, or giving comments on comments allows people to learn.

The formal organization and the formal ICT support deal with classic documents and are based on a classic client/server document management system. The informal ICT support deals with html-type documents, new expressive forms and a www-like community document system. The Internet protocol is used for the backbone. The intranet could even use synchronous multicast. Broadcast, midcast and narrowcast could be used in a synchronous and asynchronous mode, both symmetrical and asymmetrical. Rather than an infrastructure, a new (work) medium is born.

5. EDUCATIONAL COMPETENCY APPROACH

In reaction to, as well as in an attempt to extinguish the criticisms of the business environment on management institutes, many institutes have incorporated the development of managerial competencies in their programs. By doing so, they aim to make the programs more practical. Business institutes in the US and Europe have created specific courses such as entrepreneurship, management communication, presentation skills, or integrated and multidisciplinary teambuilding modules among others. Didactic strategies such as business games and simulations, group work and peer review, debates and discussions, videotaping and coaching, personal journals and real-life consulting projects are integrated in the curriculum to make business education more pragmatic.

As we have seen, the essence of the business world's criticism transcends the issue of pragmatism in business education. There are also clear business, organizational and managerial reasons to embed managerial competencies in business programs. Managerial competencies portray the different aspects of changed and changing managerial roles, for example dealing with fragmentation and perplexing paradoxes as well as daily routines. Herein lies the immediate weakness of the "mainstream" approach to managerial competencies as illustrated earlier: It is seen as a simple vehicle to increase the attraction of the program, lacking the depth of a true philosophy or clear broader framework, which indeed echoes the essence of the managerial mindset.

As we concluded in the previous chapter, it is clear that no single concept of management captures the diversity of roles and activities in which managers are involved. As executives live within fragmented and discontinuous environments, and create more complex corporate environments, they don't behave in systematic fashion. The need for a flexible strategic vision to create progress and continuous renewal, while preserving the core becomes prevalent in management. Generic, organic and changing competencies reflect the capacity of creating new businesses, core competencies, capabilities, products and services. It puts great emphasis on the capacity of individuals to continuously learn about the environment, about their performance, their objectives and capabilities, and in the light of this learning, to change, and to learn from the change. Based on this interpretation of managerial competencies, we will describe a framework and some underlying principles for an educational competency approach.

5.1. Competencies Framework

Given the way the different competency dimensions have been defined, it is clear that generic management programs like degree programs will only focus on developing generic competencies while creating an awareness about the changing competencies. An entire class of managers can apply generic competencies across organizations and different roles as they reflect the core of the managerial mindset, and of managerial and organizational life. Existing in all roles across the organization to varying degrees of importance and mastery, generic competencies refer to more abstract competencies, to an epistemology of inquiry reflecting thought processes, a theory of practice, a deeper understanding of reflective practices, and critical distance. Because generic competencies offer this continuity, business institutes can focus particularly in their degree programs on their development. As a consequence, generic competencies also have a long-term horizon. The ability to articulate a (shared) strategic vision, communicate and translate that vision throughout the organization, and enable organizational members to realize that vision is one example of a generic competency. The ability to encourage double-loop learning involves the ability to translate a managerial phenomenon to a conceptual level, come to an understanding, and translate that understanding back to a practical level, is another. But also the ability to take critical distance in order to understand managerial paradoxes, and the bundling of resources and intellectual technologies are further illustrations of such competencies.

"Changing competencies" and competencies of changeability cannot be overlooked in degree programs either. They include emerging, transitional, and maturing competencies, which refer to those competencies that have an increasing relevance and importance over the following few years (emerging), the competencies whose relevance are fading out (maturing), or competencies whose relevance may decrease while their emphasis increases (transitional). We tend to think about competencies related to technology as being the changing competencies, due to the constantly changing nature of technology. Another example could include competencies related to business development. It is important for participants and students to be aware of these time-related competencies as they are considered a source of competitive advantage connecting speed to strategic purposes, information, critical issues, and knowledge management. Also, it gives them a better assessment of the impact of the nonlinear and unpredictable fashion in which business moves rather turning away from it in a risk-averse manner.

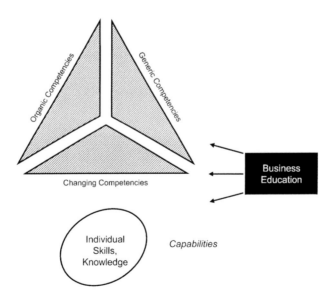

Figure 3-3. An educational competencies framework

Since organic competencies are defined as organization-specific and arising from a specific role (role-unique or context-specific), only company-tailored programs will be able to include them in their overall competency-approach. Company-specific programs can also create a more appropriate context, more specifically a learning community, in which to develop double-loop learning.

Managerial competencies are supported by capabilities. Capabilities describe the behavioral skills needed to communicate, to work as a member of a team, and to understand the dynamics of the context in which individual managers work. Capabilities such as personal effectiveness, negotiation skills, time management, team building, cross-cultural awareness, or communication skills are the foundations of competency development. As a consequence, it is important that the development of capabilities is included in the competency-approach.

It is vital that business program designers start with the development of a list of competencies. While professional literature, or research can help to develop a list of generic competencies, resources to define organic competencies can be found by investigating the company's core competencies and capabilities, its culture and philosophy, its vision and long term strategies, and the target group's role. In other words, the list of organic competencies has to portray the specificities of a particular company's business, organizational, professional, functional and managerial environments or contexts and the particular roles of the target group. Also, competency lists can only add value by their reflecting today's as well as tomorrow's manager's roles.

How can one proceed with these different dimensions and competencies? Lists of competencies tend to be quite specific: competencies should be detailed and descriptive and translated in observable, behavioral terms. Effectively using logic and data analysis to make high quality decisions, for example, can be a behavioral descriptor for decision-making. Giving candid and constructive feedback describes elements of "developing and motivating others."

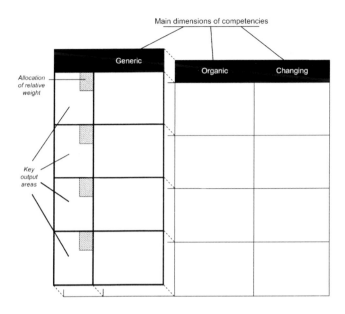

Figure 3-4. Competency Table

Then, competencies have can be clustered into key output areas, capturing a common denominator. Such a key output area could be customer orientation or business acumen. A last important element is prioritizing (for instance, by allocating a relative weight importance). Since any program only offers a limited opportunity to develop competencies, program designers will have to prioritize and only implement a few competencies and capabilities in their programs according to their particular context or niche. The focus of the program will be made clear to the (future) participant. Especially when combined with a self-development plan that starts from a customized individual competency and capability profile and the identification of the individual's learning styles, the individual can personalize the competencies and capabilities to his or her specific situation and development.

The obvious challenge, now, is how to ensure these competencies are sufficiently embedded in every person in the learning process, meaning consciously learned as opposed to innate understanding.

5.2. Specific Program Design and Program Philosophy

It is quite obvious that depending on what program design one decides on, particular capabilities and competencies will be lost or enhanced. As a result, programs will have different value. Time management and learning how to prioritize, for example, will more easily be developed in high-pressure MBA programs. In MBA programs that use one week of classes followed by one week of project and/ or preparation, such a capability will be harder to acquire. It all depends what exactly the program philosophy is and what the program wants to offer. This goes hand in hand with the well-defined theme that underlies and streamlines the whole program, as we mentioned before. This means more than just putting on a title, but a theme that really reflects the philosophy and design of a particular program.

Program design will enable the development of capabilities in support of the competencies. Given the prioritization of particular competencies, sessions can be organized to recognize, explain, develop, and experiment with these capabilities. But first, program designers will have to see what the relevant capabilities are given the list of competencies, and how they can be translated in an educational context, the learning process and sessions. These sessions can be organized parallel to or integrated in other modules for which the skill or technique is particularly relevant. Let's take the example of some sessions on argumentation, communication, and negotiation techniques to illustrate the first approach. At first, an introduction on argumentation theory is given, followed by some showcases and discussions on its relevancy and use in managerial communication. The next session then looks at argumentation theory from a methodological point of view, after which participants have to complete some assignments and read texts on critical thinking, negotiation, and the evaluation of information. A third session links argumentation and communication after which a negotiation role-play takes place. The play is videotaped so that it can be analyzed using self-confrontation techniques guided by the teacher. The last session links argumentation with negotiation techniques after which the tape is analyzed again. Also embedded into the process of the individual development plans are the feedback and extensive debriefings from peers and staff. This is a continuous effort, as the self-development path runs like a red line through the whole program.

Competencies are more closely linked to program philosophy. The program philosophy will reflect how management will be taught, and will drive the way managerial competencies are approached from a conceptual level. For instance, program philosophy will steer which competencies will take a priority and how competencies are translated into in observable, behavioral descriptors. The program philosophy will also reveal the platform that brings together knowledge and competencies. We have explained previously that many institutions have included more integrative clusters that weave together common themes from multiple and multidisciplinary angles, and action learning based consulting projects. Others use a mixture of both approaches, starting with some functional courses, and moving on to more integrative modules, then to applying integrative modules to conclude every semester or block of functional courses, or offering completely problem-based or issue-based programs. The competency approach explained here, however, is more closely related to a curriculum focusing on business processes. A focus on business processes reflects the key factors driving an organization's competitive advantage, newer management paradigms that have increasingly been pushing the business, organizational and strategic processes as the focal point of value creation and value reinvention, and new economic, organizational and managerial realities. The consequences of this focus are consistency between management philosophy, managerial roles, program philosophy, program design, managerial competencies, and the educational competency approach. As a result, the approach will offer a higher added value.

5.3.   Teaching and Pedagogical Philosophy

We stated earlier that educators should approach theories as reflections-in-action that give rise to intellectual experience by better asking pertinent questions. The result of this approach is an overall teaching philosophy in which the art of inquiry, based on working with best principles, is central. Participants can take a critical distance and search limitations. This approach offers an ability to translate a managerial phenomenon to a conceptual level, come to an understanding, and translate that understanding back to a practical level. It is especially those shifts of levels that students have to master. Remember that managerial paradoxes exactly portray a confusion or collapse of different logical levels. Even though contradictions are inferred, they aren't just referring to a simple contradiction. Paradoxes are *con-fusion*: the different levels cannot be confronted because the fusion doesn't make the differentiation of logical levels evaporate.

Learning is characterized more by interpretation than by description and analysis. It is a journey through the world in which individuals live, and through networks of meanings including aspects of self-knowledge, self-criticism, and self-development. As a consequence, teachers have to act as mentors, facilitators and helpers. At times they will have to take an almost Socratic role of dialoguing, guiding participants through the journey of dynamics, turbulences and complexities by asking pertinent questions. Within a subtle mixture of coaching, negotiated authority and learned freedom, the teacher sometimes takes responsibility for learning while sometimes this responsibility is shifted to students. Students have to be made aware of the underlying dynamic movements and look beyond the obvious and trivial. They have to learn to get close to complexities and issues, to "listen" to managerial or organizational phenomena while creating a critical distance that makes individuals reflect, and search limitations.

Consequently, the business simulations, personal journals, peer reviews, specific team building and leadership modules, multidisciplinary case studies, and computer simulations that are used to make business education more pragmatic, are not the answer. These are simply tools to create a testing and experimentation laboratory. It is important, however, that these tools serve a particular competency's development. In other words, teachers will also have to focus on the awareness, development, and assessment of that competency within the broader context of the overall aims of the program. They will have to identify appropriate tools for the competencies that were identified and prioritized. This can take place in parallel or completely integrated within particular modules.

Another element in the teaching philosophy consists of the examination of competing theories and frames of reference. This suggests a plurality of discourses and mindsets instead of reducing a student's perception to a single all-inclusive grand "master" theory, offering a more critical and integrative insight. As theories reflect networks of intelligibility, knowledge, experience and meanings, they are vehicles for searching the boundaries and limitations of knowledge. Hence, the educational community should be interested in the potential of theories to offer new possibilities.

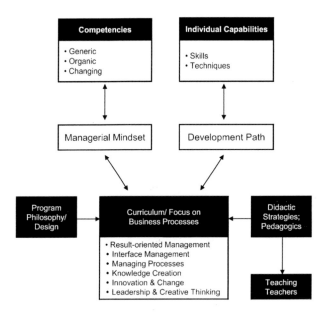

Figure 3-5. An educational competency approach

Teachers will have to get support in developing and applying such a philosophy. "Teaching teacher" seminars and the development of databases consisting of educational materials, and retaining a staff of people who have had experience in using them, can help faculty to embrace and implement such an overall teaching philosophy. Actually, it not only portrays a philosophy towards management education, teaching and learning (i.e. the pedagogical metaphor and ways to understand learning), or towards the kind of learning community that has to be created, but it also describes a managerial mindset that one wants the students and participants to develop. Support for faculty focusing on the didactic approach will also have to be ensured. For instance, as joint or co-teaching is one strategy, staff and faculty will have to coordinate efforts and have to be coached in order to find the right balance and in order to ensure open minds.

It is clear that the implementation of such a competency approach is time intensive and faculty demanding. It might even lead to the reduction of topics that are covered in a program. The added value of the competency approach, however, is also proven in reduced class sizes. That's why it is especially geared toward executive education. Last but not least, it will be important to also include an assessment congruent the competency development.

BUILDING STONES FOR THE HYBRID BUSINESS SCHOOL

- Management education can be seen as an important vehicle in developing "emergent" strategies, and managing knowledge and the organization's capabilities that drive organizational learning. Therefore, it is crucial that management education and knowledge management are harmonized.
- The dominant paradigm of management education is not entirely relevant to the needs of graduates, and hence does not prepare them for their managerial roles;
- No unique best way of teaching exists, no unique best way of learning can be identified. Learning remains very much a free act of individuals;
- Subject matter is not an objective pre-set body of transferable knowledge;
- The Hybrid Business School is founded on a combination of the travelling and growing pedagogic paradigms. The travelling metaphor advocates a more holistic and self-organizing principle. It is the learner who is in charge of his/ her learning process. The growing metaphor then brings in the personality development. Subject matter is seen as a set of experiences each student should absorb;
- We are convinced that the future of the "business school" will entail curricula focusing on business processes, progressing towards the use of a learning laboratory;
- A learning community is a vehicle for sharing experiences, information, ideas, and knowledge, for the gathering of patterns, and the bundling of resources and intellectual technologies. Within this learning community, members participate as partners in a mutual undertaking to advance learning and therein shape educational provision. Members will also find the moral and emotional support for learning;
- Technology is considered as an enabler to accelerate learning. Effective learning can only be achieved if the learning process is carefully tied to the strategic needs of the business;
- An integrated view on the working-learning-innovating triangle in a particular corporate situation, supported by an informal ICT platform, can lead to the development of a process called "community-based knowledge refinement."

REFERENCES

Allan, A. (ed.) (2002), The Corporate University Handbook: Designing, Managing, and Growing a Successful Program. Amacom.

Beck, J. (1994), The new paradigm of management education. Management Learning, 25, 2, pp. 231-247.

Brown, J. S. and Duguid, P. (1994), Organizational learning and communities-of-practice: toward a unified view of working, learning and innovation. In: H. Tsoukas New Thinking in organizational behaviour. Butterworth-Heinemann.

Business Week. (1997), Corporate America goes to school.

Business Week. (1997), When the best B-school is no B-school.

Churchill, E., Snowdon, D. and Munro, A. (eds.) (2001), Collaborative Virtual Environments. Springer Verlag.

Daniel, J. (1996), Mega-Universities and Knowledge Media. Kogan Page.

Giroux, H. and Myrsiades, K. (eds.) (2001), Beyond the Corporate University. Rownan & Littlefield Publishers.

Jarvis, P. (2000), Universities, Corporate Universities and the Higher Learning Industries: The Future for Education and Training in a Global Society. Kogan Page.

Lundberg, C. (1993), On the dilemmas of managerial instruction. Academy of Management Annual Meeting: Atlanta - August 1993.

Meister, J. (1998), Corporate Universities: Lessons in Building a World-Class Work Force, Revised Edition. McGraw Hill.

Newby H. (1999), Higher Education in the 21st Century: Some possible futures, Discussion paper, CVCP, London, March 1999.

Raelin, J. A. (2000), Work-Based Learning: The New Frontier of Management Development. Prentice Hall.

Rosenberg, M. (2000), E-Learning: Strategies for Delivering Knowledge in the Digital Age. McGraw Hill.

Chapter 4

Information and Knowledge Technologies for Virtual Education

1. INTRODUCTION

Throughout the previous chapters, we have given some insight in the processes of learning and knowledge transfer. Figure 2-7, re-introduced below as figure 4-1, shows a schematic and therefore somewhat reduced view on the processes of learning and knowledge management.

At this stage, we would like to take a more technological stance and discuss the information and knowledge technologies that support knowledge management on the one hand, and virtual education on the other. While taking this ICT view and attempting to realize and operationalize these processes with the necessary ICT support, we observe a remarkable and interesting overlap.

On a conceptual level, we will not continue to consider knowledge management and virtual education as two separate activities. The left part of figure 4-2, as argued earlier, describes (tacit) knowledge management. The right part of figure 4-2 describes virtual education. The overlap of both, proves to be the flywheel engine that brings both knowledge management and virtual education to a higher level and closer to the corporate practice, which brings both together and mutually reinforces both knowledge management and virtual education. This construction is what we will call the Hybrid Business School.

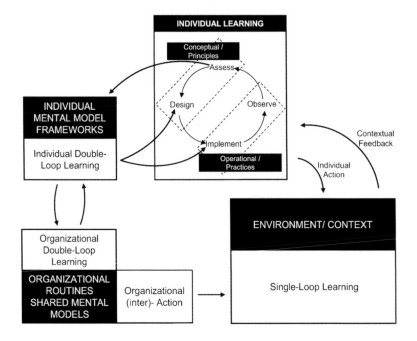

Figure 4-1. An integrated model of organizational learning

The result of this overlap is a textbook example of a "1 + 1 = 3" logic. On the knowledge management side, it allows us to deal with tacit knowledge without losing contact with explicit knowledge sharing (virtual education). On the virtual education side it allows us to offer individualized continuous life-long-learning development paths to employees, where the study material is company specific. Education has to be seen as integrated rather than specialized. In other words, our view goes against the common trend of offering more and more specialized courses. We claim that specialization is not in the best interest of companies. Management is integration, of knowledge and competencies within a given context. Just as information is meaningless without action, knowledge and competencies are powerless without a context. And technology can make education different, rather than more. This approach of virtual education goes far beyond web-based teaching in which Duke University and the University of Phoenix, to name two, have delivered outstanding programs.

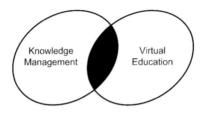

Figure 4-2. The overlap of Knowledge Management and Virtual Education

In this chapter we will introduce the information and knowledge technologies necessary and available for building the Hybrid Business School: a technology-based approach to integrated (tacit) knowledge management and continuous lifelong learning in companies. The conceptual frame on which we implement technology is shown in figure 4-3. That figure is schematized to make the goals and/or attributes and processes clearer.

Figure 4-3 focuses on the information and communication flows and attributes seen in figure 4-2. All learning is initialized via individual experiences. On the one hand, experiences interact with the individual mental models and thereby create tacit knowledge. On the other hand, experiences interact with contextual knowledge both as input and as products of its interaction. Individual mental models (images) interact with each other in order to generate shared mental models and contribute to the knowledge repository. This latter process is organized using communication platforms. The process of and interaction between experiences, tacit knowledge and knowledge repository, what is called the knowledge management process, has bridges to the contextual knowledge. These bridges attempt to contextualize some of the tacit knowledge with the aim to make it accessible to others. These bridges feed the virtual learning process with some of the individual and corporate tacit knowledge.

The process of dealing with contextualized knowledge and experiences, based on an information and communication platform, is what we call the virtual business school, depicted on the right hand side of figure 4-3. The process of dealing with experiences, tacit knowledge and the knowledge repository is what we call the "Knowledge Management Approach," depicted on the left-hand side of figure 4-3. The experiences shared between the two, the contextualization of the tacit knowledge and the interaction between explicit knowledge and experiences, all on a continuous and integrated basis, leverage the integration of knowledge management and virtual education. This leverage can only be realized if organized and developed in an adequate information and communication platform, preferably via a learning environment and learning community. Integrating knowledge technologies and learning technologies, in general, use communication technologies, like the Internet, group decision support systems, and the like.

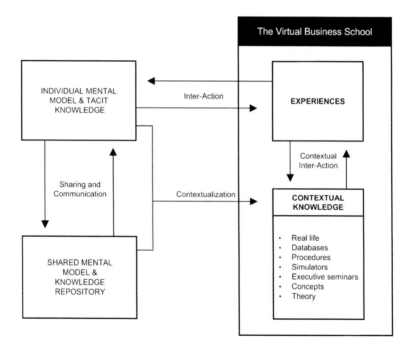

Figure 4-3. A schematic model of knowledge creation and learning

At this point, we would like to briefly introduce the more important knowledge technologies pertaining to the concept of knowledge management and virtual education.

2.   KNOWLEDGE MANAGEMENT TECHNOLOGIES

We know that creating a learning/ knowledge-based organization is a simple concept but not an easy task. A new wave of information communication technology (ICT) can support in creating knowledge-based/ learning organizations. New developments in ICT such as Case-Based Reasoning Systems (CBRS), Group Decision Support Systems (GDSS) and Artificial Neural Networks can support some aspects of organizational learning processes and organizational transformation. We can only briefly mention these technologies here.

2.1.   Case-Based Reasoning Systems (CBRS)

CBRS essentially consist of a case library and a software system for retrieving and analyzing the "similar case" and its associated information. The case library may have cases covering a broad range of ideas across different industries and business functions. Each case may contain a description to capture the underlying competitive situation, the environmental condition, management priorities, experience, values that allow a certain strategy to succeed, and moments of learning. A software system helps index each case in such a way that a search yields a modest number of "similar cases." The system can supply a complete explanation of the reasoning that has lead to each recommendation. If there is no case that exactly matches the given situation, then it selects the "most" similar case. An adaptation procedure can be encoded in the form of adaptation rules. The result of the case adaptation is a completed solution but it also generates a new case that can be automatically added to the case library.

Exposure to prior cases and experiences, and the steps taken to arrive at a decision, can often be richer and more useful as the system encodes the important learning and thinking that went into the decision. As CBRS can generate details regarding justification for particular decisions and explanations for failures, and it can be a support tool for a learning organization. It can be used as a learning device, but also as an input device for a knowledge base. Companies use this technology as a database of 'best practices.' It makes 'live experiences' accessible for others. What we are looking for is rather 'best principles.' In many respects, a CBRS is a static tool compared to a database. The use of a CBRS, however, as part of the knowledge management cycle as well as the case input of a virtual learning environment, allows us to go beyond the static situation: the process of learning and knowledge building gives rise to developing best principles.

2.2.   Group Decision Support Systems (GDSS)

Participatory management methods are increasingly gaining more interest in the corporate world.   Japanese management methods and Dutch management practice have traditionally practiced management by consensus. Consensus management has lead to a more teamwork type working environment, the formation of committees or work groups in which members share their knowledge so as to solve complex and ill-structured problems. In reference to figure 4-3, participative decision making contributes to the creation of mental models, both individual and shared, out of individual experiences. On the individual level, a GDSS can be used as a tool to help to structure a mental model or a routine, based on lived experiences. On a group level, the act of sharing and exchange allows learning as a group as well, but it also gives further input in the sense that experiences lived by others are used as input data for the creation of an individual's mental model. One can see the immediate application with sharing ideas and therefore in the creation of a group's shared mental model. This process of group learning involves the individual, and is therefore a useful tool for individual learning, but it does not focus solely on individual learning.

Participative strategy formation constitutes a learning process, as the various interest groups within an organization have different perceptions. Some group members may have more knowledge, competence and experience. Group learning occurs as the interaction among members takes place. As one member shares knowledge with the other members in the community, they gain information and knowledge. The contextual feedback instantly adds value for all involved. As each group learns and creates from its new knowledge base, the base itself also evolves. Exponential and nonlinear growth occurs with the value of each sharing group's knowledge base.

Sometimes, participative/ group planning fails due to a lack of proper participation, communication or understanding among the members in the group.   Recent developments in information technology have provided systems such as Group Decision Support Systems (GDSS).   A Group Decision Support System (GDSS) is a computer-based system consisting of software, hardware, language components, procedures and tools that can support participative strategy formation.   There can be many different configurations of a GDSS. These systems are for group planning.

A GDSS enables a group to work interactively using the networked hardware and software to complete the various aspects of the business process. For example, automated brainstorming tools can be used to address questions such as "what should the company do to become a knowledge-based/ learning company in the next five years?" Using the system, group members can generate and evaluate relevant ideas from their individual terminals. The group facilitator can then prioritize the ideas they have generated and can select one for further electronic discussion. Finally, the group can work together using a text editor to formulate a policy statement regarding the goal they have selected.

The capabilities of existing GDSS vary. Essentially, they reduce communication barriers by providing technical features such as the display of ideas, voting, compilation, anonymous input/ interaction, decision modeling, electronic mail and the bulletin board function. Also, they act as group experts by providing advice in selecting and arranging the rules to be applied during the decision making process. The ultimate aim of this technology is to bring people together and facilitate efficient and effective interactive sharing of information among group members.

Today, intranets are replacing GDSS, particularly in the function of a communication device. If the learning is focused on the decision making process, however, GDSS fulfil the purpose better than an intranet.

2.3.   Artificial Neural Networks

Artificial neural networks (ANNs) are tools derived from artificial intelligence (AI). ANNs are also part of a new information-processing paradigm that simulates the human brain. They are very strong tools in pattern finding and structuring, without any prior information. They allow for the structuring of tacit knowledge, without making it explicit, but nevertheless making it accessible. ANNs are vehicles for creating "best principles" out of "best practices." Through learning and developing an epistemology of inquiry, practices can be understood from the level of principles. When a CBRS contains many cases, and a query would generate an excessive number of cases, there needs to be a filter to break them down and summarize the cases. In essence, ANNs are instrumental in creating some tacit knowledge out of stored experiences.

In this section we want to position ANNs as learning tools within the context of Information and Knowledge Technologies (IKTs). ANNS are strong in contributing to the creation of tacit knowledge models, without making tacit knowledge explicit, but with the ability to make that knowledge potentially available for the company (see figure 4-3). ANNs fit the left (middle part) of figure 4-3. Though other advanced AI tools could be of help here, the use of ANNs has already shown successes as a knowledge generating tool to support brand-management, to visualize a change management process, or to identify client profiles. The combination of CBRS and ANN is a strong backbone for a knowledge network, particularly in light of the progression to world mass-individualization. Though ANNs lack the ability to give explanation at intermediate stages, integrating them with expert systems can somewhat remove this deficiency and therefore, they can support the learning process.

2.4. Semantic Search Engines and Link Machines

A recent and interesting development of particular use for knowledge management is what is called Semantic Search Engines. Most knowledge management technologies, including Case Based Reasoning, still need a strict organization of the data and/or cases. The quality of the search procedure relies heavily on the quality of the organization of the data and the labeling of those data. Classical search procedures use predefined labels, related to every specific piece of information. As already argued earlier, however, the problem of knowledge management precisely entails that the user does not always know exactly what he or she is looking for. Furthermore, the user doesn't always know the organization of the data.

From a user's perspective, the ideal is that one can question a knowledge base in a natural language query, which means just an everyday sentence: "Is there any experience in respect to launching new mortgage products in the last year?"; "My software product XXX doesn't operate anymore and shows the problems YYY; is there any relevant experience in this company?".

Independent of any structure, the search can be made and launched. Though the information is of course still organized in a particular way, and it could even be possible to access the same knowledge repository in a structured way, in this request the user does not need to worry about that organization.

A semantic search engine uses a kind of an overlay organization, based on keywords that are commonly used together. The search engine scans the texts that are available and that are stored using a format that allows this kind of search. Most commonly, XML is the standard for organizing text files today, increasingly and rapidly replacing HTML. Using some intelligent statistics, keywords are identified that are often used. Alternatively, for a company or branch specific database, these keywords could be given to the search engine. What the search engine does next is scan all the text in order to identify which words are often used closely together, for example. in the same sentence. If words are commonly used close together, the machine presumes that they are semantically linked. Whenever one keyword is requested, the engine will then suggest that there are a number of related keywords.

The search engine creates a semantic network of keywords, which allows translation of any given natural language query in a number of most probably related keywords. Those keywords then, can be related to pieces of text where they appear dominantly.

Once those keywords are identified, the texts are codified with the keywords, and the semantic table is made. The system is then ready for both semantic queries and semantic linking.

A minor clarification is necessary before proceeding to the practice. Other than semantic search engines, there are also pure statistical search engine that do not attempt to identify the semantics of a story. They only use observations and numerics on those observations. Most readily available search engines today use statistical search techniques. An example of what they can is the following. Do imagine asking a database for the file of "Gorge." It would probably answer that the file does not exist, but that there is a file on a guy named "George." The search engine has recognized four of the five letters in the correct position and fills in that the letter (in this the case the "e" that is "misspelled") is not of that much importance.

A semantic query is a query according to the examples given above. The system is going to respond with all those texts that come close to having a number of keywords that were either in one's request, or that are, via the semantic table, related to words in one's request. The idea of distance and proximity in meaning plays an important role here. One would ask for a specific experience with launching a particular kind of business in Poland and the system would answer that it only has cases on Hungary.

The last step in this process, and of paramount importance for knowledge management, is that once those semantic proximities are identified through a hypertext link that could be created automatically between semantically related concepts or pieces of text. In practice, that means that one only needs to store the text files in an adequate format (say XML) and that the semantic search and link engine is going to find meaning in the files and create the links between the related concepts. In other words, the semantic search and link machine organizes your information automatically in the most flexible way. In addition, one's knowledge repository is then automatically accessible for all, in such way that enables any person for his or her search request.

This recent commercially-available technology is extremely promising as a knowledge technology for any company. It is of course, equally important for the Hybrid Business School concept (as developed in next chapter). The knowledge repository (i.e. the concepts and cases) supporting learning can be organized automatically using semantic search and link machines. It can be updated easily, as it reorganizes automatically whenever a piece of information is deleted or added. Furthermore, it allows 'easy' individualization of a learning lab. For any particular participant of any particular company, a user and company specific learning can be created, by integrating information and best practices of that particular company (and even individual profile). The semantic search and link machine takes care of integrating the specific information into the already existing learning lab. In respect to the creation of corporate virtual universities, this technology is key.

3.   VIRTUAL LEARNING TECHNOLOGIES

The technology available for building a virtual learning environment is quite similar to that for a knowledge approach. In so far as the knowledge approach and the pedagogical effort reinforce each other, it is clear that the same technologies and technological platforms could be used.

Some technologies, however, are particularly beneficial developing learning environments. The best known examples are Lotus Learning Space (based on a Lotus Notes platform), Docent (a Learning Management System), Saba (an LMS with a particular focus on HR development), Blackboard (which does exactly what is says, replacing the old blackboard for the teacher) and iLearn of Oracle (with integration in the Oracle database technology), to name a few. An adequate learning environment needs to fulfill a minimum set of conditions, and it should at least produce and make available the pedagogical material in the desired pedagogical approach.

The necessary features for a learning environment can be listed as follows:

- A scheduler (agenda) for the learner, which can be managed jointly by the tutor and the student. This schedule acts as a guideline, but it also allows for monitoring of both progress and results.
- A media center of resources with hypertext links to:
  - Managerial concepts (independent from functional areas);
  - Case-studies and applications;
  - Managerial competencies (or explanations thereof);
  - Other resource material
  - (The media center should actually include multimedia such as text, pictures, movies, digital videos, etc.)
- An electronic course room for discussions and debating, question and answer sessions, and joint work, which becomes the meeting place of the knowledge-web created around the learning process (communities-of-practice). Here students, practitioners and faculty discuss topics of interest, sharing experiences, and joint work on new cases. On a purely corporate level, the diabetic community mentioned earlier, where patients, medical staff, a pharmaceutical company, and a medical insurance company exchange information and knowledge would be an example of this electronic course room.
- Profiles of students and tutors. Particularly in a virtual environment it is important to distinguish participants and their qualities so as to formulate networks or communities. As can be expected, it is difficult to work over a network with colleagues of whom you have no knowledge nor history.
- An assessment manager. The assessment manager has dual responsibility. In degree-granting courses, it is imperative to measure learning (as a diploma has to be delivered) which he/ she will do. In a personal development path, the assessment manager will work under the framework of the corporate appraisal system, and the overall human resources management strategies and policies.

The Internet (or intranet) can do one or more of the above mentioned tasks. However, integrated software has the greater advantage of promoting the integration of the environment, and the ease of use for both the student and the developer (or tutor). Integrated software takes less start-up time, and users are usually more satisfied. In theory, it is possible for a virtual school to construct its own compatible software, but in practice, this is a difficult and complex undertaking and it often prohibits a virtual school from going beyond some electronic course offerings (web-based education), or creating some discussion forum.

The database of pedagogical material should be linked to relevant web pages, with additional material, or further networks of shared interest. Links can be made between the learning environment and some interesting web sites, e.g. of the companies discussed during cases, or web sites which contain relevant up-to-date study material, taking advantage of the wealth of information on the Internet.

Video-conferencing is also an important and interesting technology. There's still a long way to go until video-conferencing is reliable enough to be optimally used for learning, but it has great potential for the future. Video-telephony, on the other hand, seems to be a very good technological tool, especially for tutoring. Today video-telephony over the Internet is still slow, yet seeing one's counterpart does add value to a conversation.

The most probable reason for the low satisfaction and limited success of video conferencing, is the dominant pedagogical metaphor, i.e. the transfer metaphor, supporting teaching via video conferencing. Video conferencing attempts to deliver, in the same inefficient way as a sit-in course, to more people in different locations. Video conferencing (or video telephony) for communication and discussion as opposed to one-way broadcasting with some questions (again one-way broadcasting), is not widely used or tried. It requires advanced and expensive technology and is not yet within easy access to the average student (be it individual or corporate). Multi-point video conferencing requires expensive and large equipment that, in turn, limits the "time and space" in which courses can be delivered. As a result, video conferencing is still rarely used. However, this situation, promises to change in the near future.

4. COMMUNICATION TECHNOLOGIES

To meet the needs of both knowledge management and management learning, an adequate stand-alone ICT environment is necessary, while communication technology is crucial. Figure 4-3 highlights the importance of communication between all different attributes. Each arrow is only realized by using communication technology. Some technological tools for communication have already been discussed, but we cannot ignore the most popular technological tool, the Internet.

Intranets, based on Internet technology, are widely used in most major companies, mainly as a tool for enhanced communication. Internet and intranets can also fulfil the role of a communication platform for our purposes, if the pedagogical material necessary for learning has been embedded. Ideally, a good learning platform should contain its own communication facility, or, if the learning platform and the communication facility are separated, they should be integrated by dynamic links (comparable to Internet hypertext links). But one can also easily make an argument for installing communication platform(s) and learning environment(s) independently from one another, which enhances flexibility and inter-operability. There is not one best practice, but rather a few possible ways to proceed. Many companies are developing communication platforms based on Microsoft Exchange or Lotus Notes. Either choice is perfect for most learning environments.

Group Decision Support Systems (GDSS, discussed before) can partly play the same role, however, they are a more restricted communication platform than the Internet.

The same can be said about chat room or bulletin board facilities that some companies may have available. It is not advisable to have a discussion platform and learning materials separated in different software environments. If there are platforms of any kind already available, one should concentrate on the functionality of that discussion forum and compare functionality to easiness of use, before taking any decision for new software.

Face-to-face communication cannot to be forgotten. Even in a virtual business school, the sit-in sessions, workshops or seminars are still important parts of the learning process. Certain aspects of a virtual business school, such as competency-driven learning, cannot be achieved in a virtual environment. Face-to-face communication proves to be most efficient and effective. Workshops, though, should concentrate on dialoguing rather than one-way communication.

As we argued previously, the changing economic and management environment supposes the development of management competencies as a crucial factor in the success of today's management. It is not uncommon to find that concepts and cases are more geared towards supporting the knowledge-based side of education, whereas different types of cases, tutorials, project work and other activities are more supportive of competency-based education. Our concept of the Hybrid Business School clearly embraces a balance between competencies and knowledge.

5. THE BIG PICTURE

The big picture of an integrated knowledge management and virtual education approach, which is designed for practicing managers, is what we call the Hybrid Business School. We will develop the concept further in the next chapter. The overlap between knowledge management and virtual education, as illustrated in the figure below, helps both act effectively, provided both are adequately supported by information technology. It is this information technology point of view – one could almost call it a technology push view – which allows us to create this "Hybrid Business School leverage" for companies. In this section we will discuss the information technologies necessary to realize both concepts and their overlapping leverage.

In the future, the integrated approach will allow for the availability of individual personal learning plans, or a mass-individualization of management education based on dynamic employee profiles and career path necessities. In the end, the main driver for the Hybrid Business School is the organization and how it deals with managing in the new economy (its philosophy, vision, strategies, managerial roles, alliances, etc.) as discussed in previous chapters. As a result, successful companies of the future will be learning organizations, whose learning aspects will be reflected in its core values, business strategy, training and development, HRD strategies, and HR policies. These elements are the continuous drivers of change and knowledge management, and will constantly update the company's management education offerings, which is where the real added value of the Hybrid Business School lies.

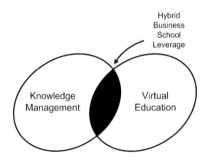

Figure 4-4. The hybrid business school's added value

The knowledge and learning potential of the Hybrid Business School approach is mainly defined by its communication. The existence of the knowledge repository, or of a CBRS, an ANN or electronic pedagogical material is a necessary condition, although not sufficient enough. Communication makes knowledge creation and exchange possible. This particular communication paradigm is different from what we traditionally know from most business schools, even from those that experiment with Internet-based courses. Although figure 4-5 depicts information technology in support of communication, it is the quality and the density of the communication that is the distinctive factor. Especially because of the important and different role communication plays in the travelling and growing paradigms.

The Hybrid Business School is founded on a combination of the travelling and growing paradigms. As discussed in the previous chapter, the travelling metaphor advocates a self-organizing principle. It is the learner who's in charge of his/ her learning process, whereas the teacher takes the role of the experienced and expert leader who guides the students through the exploration of unknown terrain. The teacher/ guide not only points out the way, but also provides navigation tools and techniques. Hence, a more holistic view and the self-organizational character of learning are emphasized. The growing metaphor then brings in the personality development. Rather than creating a body of knowledge, which would define the profession of management like the professional approach would take, subject matter is seen as a set of experiences each student should incorporate into his/her personality. As a result, communication makes the crucial difference between the power of the travelling and growing paradigms and the (mainstream) transfer paradigm. A second important difference, at least in practice, is that the transfer paradigm is often organized in functional and specialized courses whereas the travelling and growing metaphors will drive a broader and more integrated point of view.

The practice of each individual Hybrid Business School project will need a different ICT infrastructure, but figure 4-5 gives the building blocks of such a project. The more a business school or a company can build an infrastructure like the one depicted in figure 4-5, and fill it with the necessary information, the better it is armed to tackle other Hybrid Business School projects. This infrastructure offers flexibility more than anything else. If a business school can develop pedagogical material and the communication environment around it in order to run a particular degree program, they can easily and swiftly organize, for example, a two-week

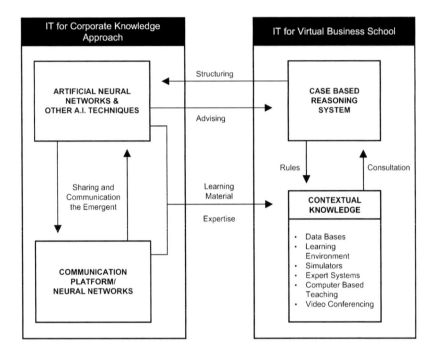

Figure 4-5. Knowledge Technologies for the Virtual Business School

BUILDING BLOCKS FOR THE HYBRID BUSINESS SCHOOL

- The process of dealing with contextualized knowledge and experiences, based on an information and communication platform, is what we call the Virtual Business School. The process of dealing with experiences, tacit knowledge and the knowledge repository is what we call the "Knowledge Management Approach";
- The overlap of knowledge management and virtual education brings both knowledge management and virtual education to a higher level and closer to the corporate practice. The Hybrid Business School mutually reinforces both knowledge management and virtual education;

- New developments in ICT such as Case-Based Reasoning Systems, Group Decision Support Systems and Artificial Neural Networks can support some aspects of organizational learning processes and organizational transformation;
- The real driver for the Hybrid Business School is the organization and how it deals with managing in the new economy, its philosophy, vision, strategies, managerial roles, alliances, and so on.

Chapter 5

The Concept of the Hybrid Business School

1.   INTRODUCTION

In this chapter, we will develop in more detail the concept of the Hybrid Business School. When we talk of the Hybrid Business School, we mainly relate to the single-loop learning cycle, depicted in the right hand side of the now well-known figure below. At the same time, the Hybrid Business School also plays an important role as enabler for organizational double-loop learning.

In other words, our concept merges knowledge creation, organizational learning, shared mental models, and individual learning. As an individual learns, changes may occur on the shared level. Knowledge is the ability to see patterns and to combine strategic resources, intellectual technologies, and processes. Hence, knowledge management aims at visualizing mental models with the aim of learning from them and sharing them, to create a learning space.

The knowledge-creating and learning organization perspectives touch all of the assumptions underlying the organization's structures and processes, and changes the roles, responsibilities, competencies and activities of all involved. Organizational learning magnifies and closes the loop of individual learning within a dynamic corporate and networked setting that allows the learning process inside a company to excel beyond efficiency frontiers. The organization's strategies, capabilities, everything from resources, (infra)-structures and support systems to enabling constraints and core philosophy will drive that organizational learning.

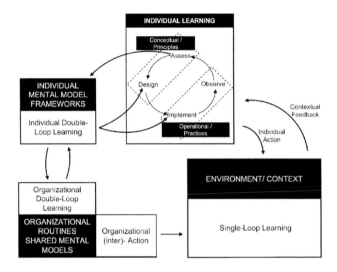

Figure 5-1. An Integrated Model of Organizational Learning

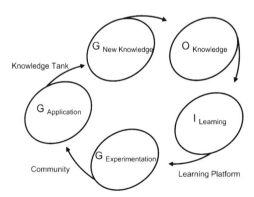

Figure 5-2. Blending knowledge creation, organizational learning and individual learning

2. THE HYBRID BUSINESS SCHOOL'S BUILDING BLOCKS

We have been taking the reader through a variety of issues related to the idea of the Hybrid Business School, reflecting the impact of the new economy on organizations and their processes, information and knowledge, managerial roles and competencies, management education and learning. We regard these issues as the building blocks of the concept of the Hybrid Business School. Let us pinpoint them again schematically in a more precise way.

- The high frequency with which radical and dramatic innovations occur have created a competitive accelerator and steeper business cycles - making time and speed crucial factors in remaining competitive and forcing companies into quantitative and qualitative leaps of improvement;
- There's a rapid transition from an industrial society into a knowledge society;
- Information is a dynamic process. Knowledge is concerned with the way one learns to fix the flow of the world in temporal and spatial terms;
- Business, markets, and organizations change in discontinuous, nonlinear and dynamic ways, allowing for the possibility of emergent and self-organizing behavior. Emergence cannot be predicted or even "envisioned" from the knowledge of what each component of a system does;
- No single concept of management captures the diversity of roles and activities in which managers are involved;
- The capacity of an organization to take effective action is based on tacit corporate knowledge. Knowledge management attempts to visualize that tacit knowledge to learn from it and share it;
- Managerial competencies better portray the particularities of managerial roles. Managerial competencies are sustained through continuous learning;
- Management education can be seen as an important vehicle in developing "emergent" strategies, in addition to managing knowledge and the organization's capabilities that drive organizational learning. Therefore, it is crucial that management education and knowledge management are harmonized;
- The dominant paradigm of management education is not entirely relevant to the needs of graduates, and hence does not prepare them for their managerial roles;

- No unique best way of teaching exists, no unique best way of learning can be identified. Learning remains very much a free act of individuals;
- Subject matter is not an objective preset body of transferable knowledge;
- The Hybrid Business School is founded on a combination of the travelling and growing pedagogic paradigms. The travelling metaphor advocates a more holistic and self-organizing principle. It is the learner who's in charge of his/ her learning process. The growing metaphor then brings in the personality development. Subject matters are seen as a set of experiences each student should absorb;
- We are convinced that the future of the "business school" will entail curricula focusing on business processes, progressing towards the use of a learning laboratory;
- A learning community is a vehicle for sharing experiences, information, ideas, and knowledge, for the gathering of patterns, and the bundling of resources and intellectual technologies. Within this learning community, members participate as partners in a mutual undertaking to advance learning and therein shape educational provision. Members will also find the moral and emotional support for learning;
- Technology is considered as an enabler to accelerate learning. Effective learning can only be obtained if the learning process is carefully tied to the strategic needs of the business;
- An integrated view on the working-learning-innovating triangle in a particular corporate situation, supported by an informal ICT platform, can lead to the development of a process called "community-based knowledge refinement."
- The process of dealing with contextualized knowledge and experiences, based on an information and communication platform, is what we call the Virtual Business School. The process of dealing with experiences, tacit knowledge and the knowledge repository is what we call the "Knowledge Management Approach";
- The overlap of knowledge management and virtual education brings both knowledge management and virtual education to a higher level and closer to the corporate practice. The Hybrid Business School mutually reinforces both knowledge management and virtual education;
- New developments in ICT such as Case-Based Reasoning Systems, Group Decision Support Systems and Artificial Neural Networks can

support some aspects of organizational learning processes and organizational transformation.

3. THE CONCEPT OF THE HYBRID BUSINESS SCHOOL

The essence of the Hybrid Business School lies in balance between two dimensions. On the one hand, there's the delivery dimension, which is the balance between virtual and nonvirtual (face-to-face) delivery and opportunities for dialogue. On the other hand, there's the content-driven dimension, exemplified by the balance between corporate knowledge management and management development strategies, more generic business, organizational and managerial processes, and the development of managerial competencies. This is exactly why we call the concept the Hybrid Business School as it is hybrid in every sense.

3.1. The Hybrid Business School's Content Dimension

The Hybrid Business School's content dimension is steered by the pedagogical metaphor on which it is based. The travelling and growing metaphors embrace self-organized learning which, as we have argued earlier, is a type of learning often observed as successful in biological colonies. As it is learner-centered, it enables learning at each individual's pace and style allowing each individual to explore in the depth and breadth necessary for that particular individual.

The Hybrid Business School perspective delivers individualized learning, based on previous knowledge and experience, and present job function and specific needs. This element directly makes learning not abstract, but contextual, as well as flexible: it happens at the appropriate time, in the appropriate dose with the proper experience so that it can be immediately applied. It pinpoints why the added value of the Hybrid Business School approach lies in the integration of corporate knowledge management, management development strategy and its activities, and human resource management. The latter refers to the way management development is embedded within a framework of a beneficial reward systems geared toward creating a learning-to-learn culture, and career development closely tied to employability, etc. A better and closer fit of knowledge management, human resource management and learning creates an upward spiral of organizational learning.

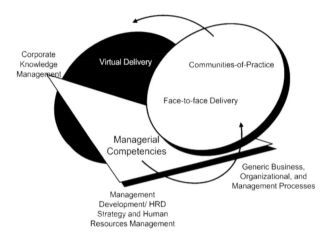

Figure 5-3. The Hybrid Business School dimensions

At the same time, our perspective embraces the nonlinearity and dynamism of learning processes. The learner carries an important part of the responsibility for the learning process as individual mental models only get created through individual learning experiences. Learning does not start from a preset and fixed body of knowledge, but enables the learner to discover management and look for the appropriate information, to form his body of knowledge, using a hypertext platform. And the learner clearly defines what is "appropriate." The hypertext platform, which we will explain more in detail later, also accommodates a multitude of learners and myriad learning paths.

3.2. The Overall Learning Strategy

We have shown that content and delivery merge in the Hybrid Business School's overall learning strategy. Central is the integrated curriculum that focuses on business, organizational and strategic processes as the focal point of value creation and business concept reinvention, a concept described earlier in this book. The integrated curriculum approach brings together the classic functions of management with actual roles and activities of managers into result-oriented management, innovation and change, etc. working towards an applied learning laboratory. This makes programs broad and deep at the same time. Broad because it integrate issues with processes, deep when the learner decides to acquire more in-depth knowledge or searches more information about particular elements. Different types of information support the curriculum design.

Laboratories are mental model practice fields, where people develop the skills to have a dialogue about their assumptions in "real time" - the moment they are dealing with an issue. This practice field enables people to talk coherently about beliefs and attitudes, to hear comments about them, to question them, and to look more clearly at (re)-sources and opportunities.

3.2.1. The Individual Learning Space

The fundamental paradigm shift we propose is that management education is learner-centered. It is the learner who's in charge of his/ her learning process. In this, subject matter is seen as a set of experiences each student should absorb.

Based on previous knowledge and experience, and present job function and roles, the learner clearly defines what is "appropriate," when, and how it is appropriate (learning style). Concretely this means that the learner will start from specific activities or questions with which s/he is confronted, within his or her particular (management) role. Learning thus becomes individually dynamic, just-in-time, just-enough, and just-appropriate. This element directly makes learning not abstract but contextual as well as flexible: it happens at the appropriate time, in the appropriate dose with the proper experience so that it can be applied.

Given the question or activity, the content is provided in different segments. As will be explained later, learners create their own dynamic between the content segments, driven by their own learning style or the way they gather information.

3.2.1.1. The Conceptual Level

First, concepts provide a common language, a learning base which reflects the minimum of what a manager should "know." S/ he should at least be able to translate a managerial phenomenon to a conceptual level, come to an understanding by asking pertinent questions, and translate that understanding back to a practical level. This is the start of developing critical distance.

To create that dynamic between conceptual and practical levels, concepts are complemented with stories and short cases. Those cases or stories are written from an experiential point of view, illustrating how concepts are applied as well as their underlying logic.

Concepts and their illustrations relate to knowledge domains that are important and relevant for a company's strategic, innovation, and other processes are part of the curriculum that will drive the conceptual learning base. The learning base can, of course, be developed in a modular way. And modules can "cascade" into different development paths. This approach offers flexibility in design, development, skill, scale, timing, and integration, and it is economically responsible.

3.2.1.2. Reflection-in-Action

Concepts detached from actual practice distort or obscure intricacies of that practice. Without a clear understanding of those intricacies and the role they play, phenomena as well as concepts cannot be well understood or enhanced. Concerned with understanding the origin, nature and validity of knowledge, this level also aims at students developing an integrative insight in managerial phenomena as well as the art of inquiry, or what we previously called a theory or epistemology of inquiry, by better asking pertinent questions. Therefore, "reflection-in-action" is enhanced through a level of actual practice that steers the development of a notion of "best principles." As we claimed before, learning cannot be abstracted from actual practice. Concepts detached from actual practice distort or obscure intricacies of that practice.

Several elements drive this "reflection-in-action" dimension. First, a segment of "guiding principles" can be linked to the cases and concepts, which guides learners through the tension between "know how" and "know why" towards a notion of "best principles." Second, and taking the step from conceptual to actual practice, a segments with tools and solutions plays a crucial role. A library of tools and solutions can consist of business simulations, templates, experiential exercises, checklists, etc. Last, in-company action-learning projects, more complex multidisciplinary case studies, or testimonials by executives are just some of the tools that can be used in action-learning and mentoring cycle. Obviously, the content created via and through the projects, case studies, and testimonials can be entered in the conceptual learning base.

Driven by its pedagogical philosophy, the travelling and growing metaphors, one of the Hybrid Business School concept pillars is the very practical management component that can only be acquired by 'doing.' Action-learning projects provide an ideal opportunity to 'exercise' management. It is based on the assumption that students learn more effectively with and from managers and teachers while all are engaged in the solution of actual, real-time and real-life problems occurring in a work setting, applying the normal business pressures and constraints of organizational realities to ensure a high quality outcome. Real life in-company project not only give the student hands-on integrative experience, but also create an immediate, visible, and tangible contribution and return on investment for the firm. Besides, project work offers a unique opportunity to assess whether the student is able to apply the knowledge he has acquired within the specific context of a particular company. For the student, the project offers the opportunity to integrate knowledge, skills and attitudes within one exercise, while teachers provide enabling constraints and take the role of experienced and expert guides who initiate and guide the students through unknown terrain that s/he needs to explore. The guide not only points out the way, but also provides navigation tools and techniques and coaches personal development.

The travelling and growing metaphors obviously also steer the teaching philosophy. Teachers act as tutors, mentors, facilitators and helpers with a subtle mixture of coaching, negotiated authority and learned freedom. In this process, the teacher sometimes takes responsibility for learning, for example, by pointing students to the knowledge base and learning material, or by directing group sessions or discussions within the learning community. Sometimes the responsibility for learning is shifted to students, for example by setting a particular pace or taking a particular approach according to the individual's learning style. Students work with their mentors and learn by observation and practice. The result is a subtle mixture of education and knowledge creation. It is in this way that the individual learner can develop an epistemology of inquiry.

The teacher/tutor also needs to assess or track the learner's progress on a continuous basis. A combination of tutor assessment and self-evaluation by the student is one possible procedure and may result in a constructive learning process for the student.

3.2.1.3. Competency Development

A further dimension concerns competency development and development of potential. It puts great emphasis on the capacity of individuals to continuously learn about their performance, their objectives and capabilities within ever-changing contexts, and in the light of this learning, to change, and to learn from that change.

As mentioned before, generic, organic and changing competencies reflect the capacity of creating new businesses and strategic resources, technologies and capabilities, and products and services. Competencies also portray the leap from information to knowledge by giving meaning to the flow information and involvement in organizational contexts. The Hybrid Business School concept adds value to corporations as it enables them to also focus on organic competencies. Unlike generic competencies that refer to more abstract competencies applied across organizations and different roles, organic competencies describe organization-specific competencies arising from a specific role (role-unique and context-specific). In other words, starting from their own tailored competency model, firms can incorporate these organic competencies into company-wide organizational development project that reflect and incorporate the core values and culture, of specific roles and strategic vision.

In addition, the educational competency approach also focuses on the development of capabilities. Capabilities describe the behavioral skills needed to communicate, to work as a member of a team, or to understand the dynamics of the context in which individual managers work. They allow people to develop and sustain competencies through continuous learning, like a genetic sequence of evolutions. This is translated, next to concepts, cases, and "guiding principles" into a fourth segment, namely a repository of competencies and capabilities linked to the other three dimensions. This repository will contain information for the learner to understand exactly why specific capabilities and competencies are related and important for the challenges and activities s/he is faced with, how they fit into the broader competency framework, and how to develop them. Hence, we create a situation whereby the repository of competencies and capabilities needed in a specific role to address particular challenges as well as a gap analysis with an individual's competency profiles, can lead to (face-to-face) competency workshops. Also, the collaborative platforms discussed below will play an important role in developing competencies and capabilities while ensuring double-loop learning.

Last, a personal development path together with personal journals complete the educational competency approach. As we saw earlier in the reflection-in-action dimension, a specific competency-mentor needs to continuously assess or track the learner's progress. A combination of tutor dialogue and self-evaluation by the student is one possible procedure and may result in a constructive competency development process for the student.

3.2.2.   The Collaborative Learning Space

A second important aspect is the collaborative learning space, consisting of a learning laboratory or collaborative forum, and communities-of-practice.

As we saw before, the integrated curriculum design focusing on business, organizational, and managerial processes will work towards the use of such a learning laboratory. This forum is a true "safe" peer-to-peer, issue-driven platform for collaboration, dialogue and experimentation. It enables people to talk coherently about beliefs and attitudes, to hear comments about them, to question them, to look more clearly at sources and principles, to reflect upon them, and to experiment with and apply them. The collaborative forum widens this perspective somewhat, making it more than just a group session. Program heads, faculty, executives, advisory boards, corporate action-learning sponsors, and students mutually engage in developing new understandings, approaches and unbounded sets of perspectives. This peer learning proves to be very efficient and interesting. Guided by a tutor, participants can experiment and apply newly acquired knowledge, behaviors and competencies. This type of forum can be organized both virtually and face-to-face. Members will also find the moral and emotional support for learning, helping participants to become continuous learners.

Second, communities-of-practice, or networks of practitioners are another important item of this collaborative learning space. Offering an integrated view on working, learning and innovation around particular issues or challenges within a particular corporate context and community in which the work actually takes place, communities-of-practice are significant sites of sustained individual learning.   As with learning laboratories, communities-of-practice can be organized virtually and face-to-face. Alumni can play an important double role in such communities: one of provider of experience, i.e. as expert, and one of continuous learner. And because of its inherent flexibility, the Hybrid Business School facilitates in this dynamic life-long affiliation and membership of such communities-of-practice.

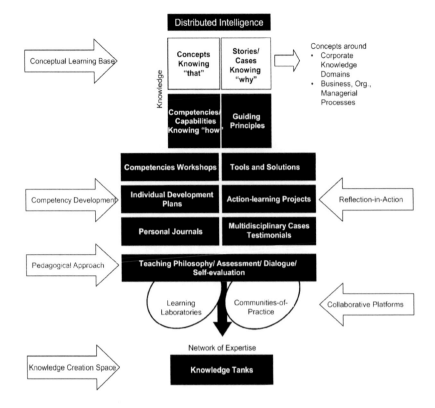

Figure 5-4. The Hybrid Business School's overall learning strategy

At the same time, these communities-of-practice also enable organizational double-loop learning to take place as they bring together mental models in a community's "way of seeing". From a corporate point of view, the Hybrid Business School based management education effort magnifies the firm's knowledge base as well as the knowledge network. Therefore, the Hybrid Business School should always coincide with the corporate knowledge management effort. The Hybrid Business School is an important vehicle through which continuous learning, knowledge-creating and innovation processes can occur That dynamic learning process aims to enhance individual and corporate learning, and not just to transfer ideas/knowledge during one learning moment. And again, the learning base can benefit from content created throughout the discussions in the learning laboratories and communities-of-practice.

3.2.3. Collaborative Knowledge Creation Space

The Knowledge Tank is the last pillar of the Hybrid Business School concept, and takes the collaborative aspect even further. The knowledge tank is a peer-to-peer, issue-driven, both virtual and face-to-face platform aimed at establishing a continuous knowledge-creating process. The knowledge-creating process is driven by interest groups (knowledge spaces) that focus on a limited number of new issues, concepts, and challenges.

Again, faculty, executives, advisory boards, corporate action-learning sponsors, and alumni can play an important double role in such communities: one of provider of experience, and one of driver of a knowledge creating process. The knowledge tank concept allows participants to talk and cohesively pursue completely new issues and insights. In other words, it goes a step further than the communities-of-practice in the sense the latter start from existing issues, comment them, question them, and look more clearly at sources and principles. The knowledge tank widens this perspective as its objective is to generate a "creative thinking environment" in which new ways of thinking and acting are discussed, future paradigms and principles are explored, strategic as well as operational concepts and their underlying logic are tested, and resources and networks defined.

Each knowledge tank can work during a set time in order to observe, analyze, evaluate and define new concepts, illustrations, guiding principles, competencies and capabilities, tools and solutions. Tutors drive the process, experts can be instrumental in conducting background research, in compiling and organizing information. The output of all these thinking exercises should be of direct benefit to the organization and its learning base. Hence, we feel that it is of symbolic importance that the knowledge tanks deliver their findings during a small "World Economic Forum"-like event, ensuring efficient double-loop learning. It is clear that such events are not simply a one-shot opportunities; each knowledge tank has to be seen as a continuous cycle around a continuum of events in time.

3.3. The Hybrid Business School's Delivery Dimension

We consider learning to be a dynamic process of continuous advancement, experience and growth. Learning gives the opportunity for individuals to pause, reflect upon and reframe issues and experiences not only from their own insights, but also in relation to the interaction with others. Learning styles and pace will be important individual drivers. In any case, learning is not abstract but contextual: it happens at the appropriate time, in the appropriate dose with the proper experience so that it can be immediately applied. As such, learning can be seen as the process whereby knowledge is created through the transformation of experience, "know that," "know-how" and "know-why."

3.3.1. Pedagogical Material

The learner is the focal point in the process of learning. It is the learner who searches for issues, looks for the appropriate information, comes up with questions, and thus "discovers" management. Through activities and questions s/he is challenged with, the learner clearly defines what is "appropriate." Hence, the student's overall aim is also to focus on cultivating his/ her personality. The student is pictured as a garden in which everything is already planted, but which still needs to grow.

We used the metaphor of a motorbike earlier. On a motorbike, as Pirsig argues, the driver is part of nature. He feels and smells nature and is able to react much faster to changes in nature. This analogy suggests that learners have to be in touch with the environment - riding their bike - in order to experience a close feeling for things and their backgrounds. As we are talking about a dynamic movement, learners should pay attention to their surroundings and remain alert. When we have seen, we travel and grow, hence we learn.

In other words, the learner develops and designs his "own" body of knowledge using his own learning style. Technology, such as hypertext platforms, enables this process as it allows learners to create an individual dynamic between the four segments, namely concepts, illustrations, guiding principles, and competencies. The hypertext platform, which we later will explain more in detail, not only offers that flexibility, but also accommodates a multitude of learners and myriad learning paths. It produces new realities, new meaningful contexts with their own particular "grammar," and thus creates a unique management rhetoric for the student.

The pedagogical material, therefore, is organized differently than classical functional textbook format in order to accommodate the hypertext platform. The electronic form alters only the delivery, but it also reflects the overall learning strategy depicted earlier. Subject matter is seen as a set of experiences each student should absorb.

The concept library provides a common language for understanding, a learning base which reflects the minimum of what a manager should "know." The library, however, will have to be developed in such a way that it fits the logic of the integrated curriculum.

The case/ illustration library may include cases covering a broad range of ideas across different industries, company-specific issues, organizational processes, or a combination thereof. Each case illustrates an in-depth experiential description to capture the underlying elements that have driven a certain strategy, decision, policy or process. This makes the cases more than just anecdotal as they offer a deeper conceptual ground by showing how concepts were applied (know-how) as well as the underlying logic (know-why). Given the hypertext approach, these cases will only be used when relevant to the student and hence related to a specific challenge with which they are faced at that particular moment. The link to the case-based reasoning system discussed in the previous chapter is clear. Such a system helps index each case so that learners can look for "similar cases", or it can generate details regarding justification for particular decision, explanation for failures, and the logic behind decisions made. If there is no case that exactly matches the given situation, then it selects the "most" similar case. An adaptation procedure can be encoded in the form of adaptation rules. The result of the case adaptation is a completed solution but also the generation of a new case that can be automatically added to the case library. Consequently, it can be used as a learning device, but also as an input device for a knowledge base. That process of learning and knowledge building gives rise to developing best principles. Working with principles teaches participants to develop a conceptual reading and cohesive mindset about management and a theory of practice, providing them with broader powers of strategic analysis.

This is further put into practice in our next segment of activity learning. Within the hypertext platform, this segment refers to tools and solutions in which the student will be actively involved, enabling him to translate a managerial phenomenon to a conceptual level. He can then come to an understanding by asking pertinent questions, and translate that understanding back to a practical level, in other words, developing critical distance.

The last segment of competencies and capabilities adds to this. It offers the learner information about the competencies and capabilities involved, which can then be compared to an individual competency profile or potential profile. Through a gap analysis and eventually a tutor's feedback and guidance, the learner can engage in a competency workshop. In a broader frame, there is a clear link to action-learning projects, communities-of-practice and competency development. The development of competencies plays an important role as students are able to create knowledge from information.

The hypertext platform (the Internet is the perfect illustration) allows users to inter-link elements from the four segments, using their own strategy and learning path, given the individual's particular context. These inter-linkages can be on a horizontal level (i.e. within segments), on a vertical level (between segments), or a combination of both. For example, when a student reads a text about one concept and encounters a reference to another, he/she can link up to information about the other concept with a simple click of the mouse. The same is true with the case and illustration library. When a student reads a text about a concept, a link can be made to a case that illustrates the application of that concept. Similarly, a text about a company case should provide links to any concept that is mentioned or to some activity learning exercises or a repository of competencies.

This allows a learner to focus on exactly what interests him/her, and thus enhances learning possibilities. It is, of course, the role of the tutor to organize material in such a way that it makes complete sense in terms of the particular target group. It would be unrealistic to think that any Hybrid Business School could ever produce material that perfectly contextualizes a company's and individual's environment.

On the other hand, the hypertext format enables fast, continuous development and adaptation of the case library (or any of the other libraries) without having to alter the other segments at the same time. With the rapidly changing economic and business realities, the electronic platform adds value to companies and individual participants. We're describing a dynamic system in which the different segments and dimensions each also have their own dynamic and pace. Dynamics are driven by the company's approach to knowledge management and organizational learning, the corporate strategy, philosophy and vision, the strategic use of management development initiatives, and the development of subject matters and management itself.

3.4. The Hybrid Business School's Main Technology Pillars

The Hybrid Business School environment can only be realized with considerable ICT effort. ICT, however, is a tool and not an end in itself. Consequently, our focus is using the appropriate technologies driven by strategic instinct, performance improvement, communities-of-practice, and especially, human design. It is ICT that accommodates the individual and not, as so often can be found, the individual that has to accommodate the ICT system design. This approach is what some people would refer to as a Japanese mindset for using information technology.

The Hybrid Business School environment has been developed on several technology pillars including Internet, digital content management, filtering and search facilities, Knowledge Management/ core engine, and virtual learning, communication and pedagogical technologies.

3.4.1.   Internet

There are numerous advantages to using the Internet as the communications medium. The virtual nature of the Hybrid Business School and the necessity of interactively reaching a large number of individuals (regardless of place and time) can only be achieved through the Internet. The central entrance point for all parties will be an Internet portal.

For individual coaching, workshops and communities, standard available components can be used for posting messages and replies, interactive discussions, meetings, presentations, video sessions, etc.

3.4.2.   Content Management

The strength and success of Hybrid Business School depends greatly on a strong knowledge base and efficient digital content management. It is imperative to integrate a robust and high-performance system to gather, tag, index, model, store, manage, and publish content in a learner-specific manner within the portal.

Data objects form documents (text, audio and visual) that in turn are stored within related folders. By using such hierarchical structuring, data objects can then be indexed accurately. This structuring also offers a number of advantages, such as the ability to dynamically compound (temporary) content, and allowing multiple ways of searching and retrieving content while enabling to map content data. It also optimizes the way in which data can be indexed automatically, be stored in/ on different types of media and the way content is published through the learning portal. The semantic search and link engine, described in the previous chapter, plays an important role in this organization.

3.4.3. Information filtering and multimedia search facilities

Intelligent information retrieval plays an important role within the Hybrid Business School and is fully integrated with digital content management, previously discussed.

Both the Hybrid Business School and its users have many internal and external sources that produce and store data. Through unlocking, structuring and aggregating these resources and the data contained within them, it creates a precious asset that enlarges the value of an organization's human capital. The multimedia search and retrieval component in the Hybrid Business School automatically searches and indexes data stored on sources such as file servers, Internet/Intranet, databases and in groupware systems. Once the data is compared with the ontology of the Hybrid Business School's knowledge domain, it can be filtered to produce relevant information. In this way, repositories of corporate knowledge are built up.

Semantic search and link engines can play a very powerful role here. Not only are they instrumental in the organization of the content, but independent of that organization, they allow individuals to query the knowledge domain in an almost complete free format. For the time being, semantic search engines are limited to text files, though experimental software exists to search semantically on speech and video. Those products would offer a solution for searching spoken video clips.

3.4.4. Linking learner's profile to content, performance and assessment: The Hybrid Business School's core engine

Perhaps the most crucial part of the Hybrid Business School platform is its matching function. As previously described, an individual learner's curriculum based on previous knowledge and experience, and present job function and roles, is created dynamically. The learner clearly defines what is "appropriate," when and how it's appropriate (learning style). Concretely this means that the learner will start from specific activities or questions s/ he is confronted with in his or her particular (management) role. A resulting learning profile determines his or her curriculum and which information in the Hybrid Business School knowledge base is, or could be of relevance to him of her. The information is automatically structured and delivered as learning content, in the appropriate form, to the learner. This is carried out by the combined functions of the platform's content management system and information retrieval engine.

Yet, in order to guarantee that learning material matches the learner's abilities and expectations, his or her performance and progress must continuously be assessed and tracked. A combination of tutor dialogue and self-evaluation by the student is one possible procedure and may result in a constructive development process for the student. These measurements, however, must have a high degree of accuracy. To attain this, the Hybrid Business School will have to use methods that analyze and weigh the results and feed them back to the system and the learner's profile.

To produce the functional enhancements that are necessary, we will use a combination of Case Based Reasoning Systems (CBRSs), which essentially consist of a case-library and a software system for retrieving and analyzing the "similar case" and its associated information, and Artificial Neural Networks (ANNs), simulating the human brain. Although other advanced AI tools could be of help here, the use of ANNs has already shown success as a knowledge-generating tool to visualize a change management process, or to identify client profiles. The combination of CBRS, expert systems, intelligent agents, and ANN provides a strong backbone for a knowledge network, particularly in light of the progression to mass-individualization.

Those technologies all have the same goal, namely to bring the content semantically closer to any individual learner. The choice between those technologies depends on how much information is available on the learner's behavior, as well as the amount of effort (and money) that can be made available for continuous tracking and tracing of the learning process. The most interesting technologies are the kind of smart search engines that keep track of earlier searches and that explore links. Therefore, they can bring those parts of knowledge that are more relevant for the learner closer to that learner. Semantics then support content filtering. These technologies are sometimes labeled as "butler technology." Experimentation with other AI technologies like ANNs is promising in order to elicit dynamic 'client' profiles, in this case dynamic learner profiles. Although these technologies are still experimental and expensive, they will become increasingly dominant in the future.

3.4.5. Virtual Learning Technologies

A number of the necessary features for a learning environment are listed as follows:
- A scheduler (agenda) for the learner, which can be monitored and managed jointly by the tutor and the student.
- A multimedia resource center with hypertext links to:

- Managerial concepts (independent from functional areas);
- Case-studies, stories, illustrations;
- Managerial skills and competencies (or explanations thereof);
- Best practices, guiding principles;
- Other resource material;
- An electronic course room for discussions and debating, question and answer sessions, and joint work, which becomes the meeting place of the knowledge-web created around the learning process (communities-of-practice).
- Profiles of students and tutors. Particularly in a virtual environment it is important to distinguish participants and their qualities so as to formulate networks or communities.
- An assessment manager. The assessment manager has dual responsibility. In degree-granting courses, it is imperative to measure learning (as a diploma has to be delivered) which he will do. In a personal development path, the assessment manager will work under the framework of the corporate appraisal system, and the overall human resources management strategies and policies.
- Links to outside software (e.g. HRM software).

3.4.6.   Communication Technologies

To meet the needs of both knowledge management and management learning, an adequate stand-alone IT environment is necessary, while communication technology is crucial.

Intranets are widely used in most major companies, mainly as a tool for enhanced communication. Intranets can also fulfill the role of a communication platform for our purposes, if the pedagogical material necessary for learning has been embedded. Ideally, a good learning platform should contain its own communication facility, or, if the learning platform and the communication facility are separated, they should be integrated by dynamic links.

Video-conferencing and video-telephony also have to be included as important communication technologies.

3.4.7.   Pedagogical Technologies

Lotus Learning Space or Oracle's iLearn are among those platforms that can be used as a pedagogical software environment. In addition to the hypertext database, these platforms produce new releases offering more flexibility and more possibilities for integration.

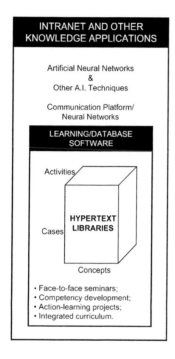

Figure 5-5. The Hybrid Business School's technology pillars

3.4.8.   Collaborative technologies

Collaborative tools available today commercially cover a wide range of electronic discussion room technologies, including video contact, voice over IP, electronic boards for written discussions, and asynchronous discussion forums. The availability of broadband telecom networks is an absolute must for the video link tools. Unfortunately, those networks are not yet commercially available and accessible for all at economically justifiable prices. And practice shows that as learners and tutors become more familiar with available technologies, their use will become more widespread.

We feel that collaborative software, integrated within the learning platform, is the best choice.

3.5.   Pedagogical Concerns and Non-virtual Delivery

Presenting pedagogical material in an electronic format is appropriate in terms of applying the travelling and growing metaphors, which form the basis of the Hybrid Business School's pedagogical philosophy. The general setup of the concept is well complemented by a system that allows tutors and students to easily access and isolate those concepts relevant to themselves. This is the main advantage of the electronic format over the textbook format.

Typically, business schools use ICT as an alternative to a traditional classroom setting in order to reduce their marginal costs. ICT has, however, often been unsuccessful as a learning delivery method since it still supports the traditional delivery paradigm (the transfer theory). ICT here plays the role of intellectual crane filling the empty vessel. As argued earlier, the use of ICT to support the transfer metaphor only magnifies its weaknesses.

Any use of ICT, particularly in terms of learning technologies, should be based on the conversational paradigm reflected by the travelling and growing metaphors. Here, knowledge here is shaped by the tools of inquiry and therefore by conversation, emphasizing the important role of tutorials. It is this focus on conversation that makes the Internet such a success. The Hybrid Business School hypertext approach is based on that Internet technology concept. Tutorials, projects, communities-of-practice, knowledge tanks, and face-to-face events should reinforce that conversational paradigm.

SUMMARY

- A Hybrid Business School delivers flexibility in time and space but also in the discovery of the management field. Hence, it is oriented towards the manager who is looking for the appropriate knowledge and education.
- A Hybrid Business School approach is built on the acceptance that different types of knowledge contribute to developing managers.
- A Hybrid Business School delivers individualized learning, based on previous knowledge and experience, present role and specific needs. It also allows for different forms of learning and different aspects of what should be learned.
- This necessitates a particular pedagogical approach, different from the still prevailing one-way broadcast delivery. The Hybrid Business School's focal point is learning as opposed to teaching. The pedagogical approach we embrace is learner-centered, and the learner carries an important part of the responsibility for the learning process (self-organized learning).
- A Hybrid Business School environment allows for nonlinear dynamic learning and flexible learning alternatives.
- A Hybrid Business School offers integrated learning. Management is not the addition of different disciplines. Education should not be functionally driven but competency driven. A project-based approach completes this offering.
- A Hybrid Business School creates most of its added value since it is integrated with the knowledge management approach of the company as well with the human resources management and management development strategies.
- A Hybrid Business School integrates virtual and nonvirtual delivery. Learning cannot only be virtual.
- A Hybrid Business School responds to both the necessity for a company to create its own corporate university and the necessity for such a university to keep an outward look.
- In a Hybrid Business School, competencies are as important as a good knowledge base.
- A Hybrid Business School relies heavily on the introduction of communities-of-practice, a network of practitioners, and knowledge tanks, that aim at generating knowledge-creating processes.

Chapter 6

Illustrations and Examples of Hybrid Business Schools

1. INTRODUCTION

Since we have explained the building blocks and the concept of the Hybrid Business School, it would be beneficial to discuss some concrete examples. We have chosen the term Hybrid, because the Hybrid Business School blends the corporation's knowledge management approach with strategy, performance, individual development, business, management, and organizational processes, and it also merges a virtual (on-line) delivery with face-to-face workshops. The need for the latter not only stems from experiences with virtual delivery, but is also a direct consequence of the learning and the educational competency-based approach we have advocated in this book.

The content of the workshops, being driven by roles, activities, and devising answers, as well as the teaching method is very different from what we know today in most classroom situations. Moreover, in the appropriate learning-to-learn culture, the Hybrid Business School will create an upward spiral of organizational learning for the corporation in which a Hybrid Business School project is developed.

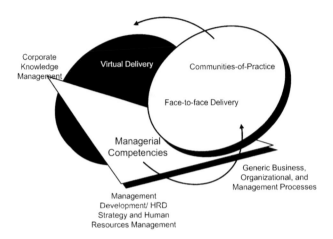

Figure 6-1. The Hybrid Business School dimensions

It is clear that one doesn't need the complete Hybrid Business School platform or approach in order to make a particular learning project successful. It depends on whether you are organizing a degree program offered to an open market, a company-specific degree program, or a corporate management development initiative that is part of a broader training and development or HRD strategy. For companies aiming to move rapidly into the knowledge era, however, the infrastructure described in the previous chapter may prove to be an important basic condition, a necessary but not yet sufficient condition.

In the next paragraphs we will give an example of a corporate learning project as well as an illustration of two degree programs. Our concept is not built by just hitting one home run. It is constructed with a particular philosophy in mind, consistently hitting singles, doubles, triples, and home runs before, during, and after the start.

2.   A CORPORATE HYBRID LEARNING PROJECT

One example can be drawn from a European-American telecommunication network services firm, offering pan-European and trans-border customized network solutions for voice, data, video, graphics service levels, and bandwidths. First, the firm experienced a very steep and fast growth curve with the consequent rise in the number of employees. Most staff members were highly skilled and educated. Second, the nature of the technology, the complexity of the solutions offered, and the fact the firm tried to create a complete new business, required a high learning curve for the organization and its stakeholders. Hence, an HRD strategy that served individual development opportunities as well as the growth processes was required.

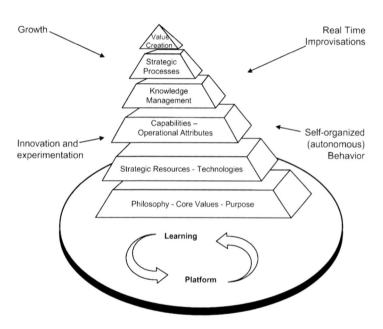

Figure 6-2. Challenges for a corporation's learning project

Senior management understood already in the early stages of growth that the company not only needed a well-defined knowledge management approach, but also that its organizational development had to be built on strategic resources and technologies, and capabilities that were flexible enough to change over time. They felt it was important to build a culture and philosophy based on a small set of values in order to offer continuity within the turbulence of continuous change and discontinuity. The HRD strategy had to support and transcend these challenges.

Let's make some of these elements more concrete. First of all, a small set of general guiding values and principles - the first part of the core philosophy - was defined during a number of workshops with senior and middle management. As Collins and Porras advocate, these values were seen as the organization's essential and enduring beliefs, not to be compromised for financial gain or short-term expediency. Next, we defined the second part of the firm's philosophy, the core purpose, which is the organization's fundamental reason for existence, like a guiding star on the horizon. The outcome of the exercise for this company is shown below.

Values:
- Lead the European network services revolution;
- Amaze our customers with our reliability, quality, and willingness to customize networking solutions;
- Empower creative individuals.

Purpose:
- "Complexities made simple"

The impact of this philosophy on the organization is enormous. For example, contracts with staff, suppliers, and clients are more transparent and is simplified. The firm is much more careful of underlying technical issues for customers, partners, and shareholders. Further, the philosophy guides the operating practices, business processes and the organizational structure. In short, the whole business and product concept is guided by and assessed according to the "complexities made simple" purpose.

The firm's knowledge management approach is organized around focus groups. These focus groups consist of people from different departments involved in a similar issue, for example, relating to business development or to customer support. Let's concretely go into the last example. The customer support center assists customers with a help desk that is accessible 24 hours a day, 7 days a week, and is the single point of contact for customers seeking technical information or problem resolution. It is also responsible for informing customers of maintenance and upgrade activities. Using an IT-based support system that is shared by the customer support center, the network operations center, or representatives in key-cities throughout Europe, direct feedback on the status of service and technical information can be given to customers.

This focus group also has access to a knowledge management system that consists of two main parts. First of all, the system aims at creating knowledge. Members of the focus group therefore develop (electronic) stories of customer challenges and issues, and point out how they were handled. Templates are available to simplify this work and they point out the practices and principles behind them. These stories are then screened by peers and retained as complete new cases, or added as additions to existing stories. The story-approach was chosen because stories enable employees to understand complicated issues in an accessible and intelligible way. Second, the system is geared towards sharing this knowledge. A search capability was added to the system so that members of the focus group can at all times access the knowledge data base in order to search for similar issues and for people who were involved in these earlier stories. The system works like a central communication hub so that members don't have to reinvent the wheel time after time, and enables them to offer a smoother service to the customer, thereby saving time and increasing internal efficiency.

Once this direction was taken, senior management created an environment to encourage employee knowledge sharing. The Human Resources department consequently developed processes and policies that encouraged and rewarded employees to invest in a life-long learning path and consistently share their gained knowledge with others. Senior management seriously backed this initiative. Also, the HR department developed a company-specific competency-model, together with a tool enabling employees to check for the competencies and knowledge they lacked or needed to improve. The competency model is also used as a tool for concrete measurement for evaluations linked to compensation and benefits. New hires were screened for their desire to learn and transfer knowledge. The focus groups were given the role as the guardians of maintaining an "out-of-the-box thinking" and "exploring the boundaries of the unknown" culture.

The HRD department was branded as a "Eurobrand" business center, a high priority strategic leader and business partner with ample resources which looked for strategic alliances with European business schools. This clearly portrayed the function of HRD as that of creating and deploying coherent programs on a Pan-European level, and offering customized solutions for individuals and focus groups. HRD is the owner of the European HRD processes, initiating programs and courses, establishing standards, identifying providers, monitoring quality, providing information, internal marketing, and managing logistics and enrollment. The focus groups and senior management are seen as contributors and influencers in that process, as well as coaches to employees and first-line managers. Within the Hybrid Business School concept, they will also act as communities-of-practice. The HRD department appointed an outside consultant to help in the development of the HRD strategy, coordinate the role-out of the corporate learning center, and later on to act as the intermediate between the company and the different educational partners.

The corporate strategy and vision, the business future, the big picture, and employability all drive the HRD strategy, a strategy based on one competency model linked to roles and activities and three "levels" of complexity. Employees can participate in a number of topics in each level, and in this way follow a horizontal path. At the same time, learners can choose a vertical path by digging deeper in particular related subjects. In other words, the three levels blend into each other.

First, the initiating level of complexity describes topics at a relatively basic level. Next is the managerial competency level with a supplemental personal learning plan. For this, some generic and organic competencies as well as some capabilities were specified within the corporate model. Existing in all roles across the organization to varying degrees of importance and mastery, generic competencies refer to more abstract competencies, like a reflective mindset and a deeper understanding of managing oneself, to collaborative and analytic practices, critical distance and contextual challenges. The ability to articulate a (shared) strategic vision, communicate and translate that vision throughout the organization, and enable organizational members to realize that vision is one example of a generic competency. The ability to encourage double-loop - learning involving the ability to translate a managerial phenomenon to a conceptual level, come to an understanding, and translate that understanding back to a practical level - is another.

"Changing competencies" and competencies of changeability include emerging, transitional, and maturing competencies, which refer to those competencies that have an increasing relevance and importance for the future (emerging), the competencies whose relevance are fading out (maturing), or competencies whose relevance may decrease while their emphasis increases (transitional). For this particular company, competencies related to network and telecommunications technologies and competencies related to the changing customer demands and the changing business structure were included. A number of capabilities were also covered by the competency track. Capabilities such as personal effectiveness, negotiation skills, time management, team skills, cross-cultural awareness, or communication skills were seen as fundamental.

Again, a horizontal as well as vertical path can be distinguished. Also, it is clear that the different competencies are intertwined by the content driven topics. The company deemed it important that competencies portray the leap from information to knowledge by giving meaning to the flow of information within organizational contexts.

The final complexity level deals with strategic issues to future business and an action mindset of organizational change dynamics. Topics within this level can be linked to each other, and learners can also gain a deeper insight into topics by moving from one level to the other. Of course, the hypertext enables and allows learners to "play" between the different levels, and between concepts, cases, and activities.

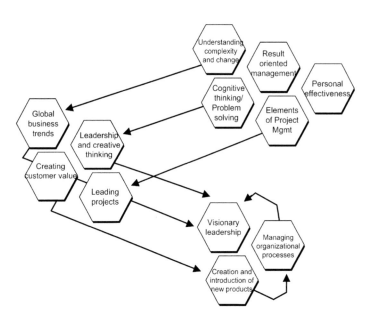

Figure 6-3. Highlight of the firm's HRD strategy

Within each level, a number of modules have been defined. Each theme or module is characterized by three red lines, namely a "big picture", organizational, and personal theme. This means that all concepts, cases, and activities are presented in the context of these three themes.

Figure 6-3 exemplifies one such module that also portrays a clear path of development for the employees.

Consequently, a "Hybrid Learning Center" was initiated. Catchy Lotus Notes pages were used for internal marketing and to provide information about learning objectives, content, didactic approach, background of the tutors, prerequisites, and so on, accommodating once more the self-learner approach. It is the learner who develops and designs his "own" body of knowledge using his own learning style.

Electronic versions of the competency-assessment tool and personal learning plan were also provided. Once an individual's competency model is made, the employee discusses it with a coach who guides him or her towards a particular learning track. As employees advance in the organization, their competency needs and personal learning plan change. This immediately supports the learning mindset in the organization, and makes self-education a strategic process written into the overall organizational processes. The process also helps the employee understand his or her strengths and weaknesses and the direction he or she may take within the organization. Focus group managers play a role as well in this guidance process. In addition to their guidance input, they review which action-learning projects could provide an ideal opportunity for the employee to "exercise" management. And finally, in combination with the ongoing assessment during the individual learning sessions, there is both a self-evaluation and a tutor assessment.

The company next set up learning management system including electronic enrollment, follow-up and follow-through. They also identified, acquired, or developed business simulations, personal journals, action-learning in-company projects, multidisciplinary case studies and illustrations, experiential exercises, and an activity learning set (tools, applications). Starting from roles, activities were listed based upon which topic and subject matters were identified to initiate the building of a concept or principal library. The cases and illustrations covered a broad range of ideas and in-depth descriptions of the "know-how and know-why" about different industries, economic trends, company-specific issues, organizational processes, or any combination thereof. Also, an artificial, intelligent, flying "learning consultant" was conceptualized who gave the learner additional information, navigated him through the content, and introduced short self-assessments.

For each module, program heads, faculty, senior managers, in-company action-learning project sponsors, and students were brought together virtually and face-to-face in a learning laboratory. That laboratory allowed people to have a dialogue about their assumptions in "real time" - in the moment they were dealing with an issue. This practice field enabled people to talk coherently about beliefs and attitudes, to hear comments about them, to question them, and to look more clearly at sources and opportunities. In addition, the focus group to which the participant belonged, acted as a community-of-practice. This community-of-practice will play an important role in developing competencies as it brings together the "know-how" and "know-why" with concrete possibilities for on-the-job application, and at the same time, ensure double-loop learning. The key to success is a clear support and active involvement of every member of the focus groups. Consequently, the firm initiated a number of small learning exercises and learning competition for the various focus groups to support the learning culture and show the advantage for all involved.

As a last element, senior management defined a number of issues and ventures that were crucial for the company's future. Trend analysis linked to future key elements of products, service, and delivery geared towards creating customer value, technological innovations and new business models, and cultivating internal growth were some of the issues and ventures of knowledge tanks. Around these issues, several knowledge tanks were initiated. Internal experts joined with external experts to drive research and discussions while alumnae of the learning experience and learning laboratories focused on creating new knowledge and experiences around these issues. An event was planned after which new knowledge tanks would be derived from the outcome, in order to restart a new knowledge-creating cycle.

3. TWO DEGREE PROGRAMS BASED ON THE HYBRID BUSINESS SCHOOL CONCEPT

Our other real case studies offer a different angle, namely that of degree programs. The first case illustrates the development of a degree program at the Euro-Arab Management School (EAMS) in Granada, Spain. The second case illustrates the development of a Master in Business Innovation and Intrapreneurship (MBI&I) program at Nyenrode University, the Netherlands Business School.

3.1. The Euro-Arab Management Diploma of EAMS (Granada, Spain)

EAMS is a project of the European Union and the Arab League, supported by the Spanish Government. Emerging from the Euro-Arab dialogue as a way to further develop economic relations between Europe and the Arab World, EAMS is mentioned in the Action Program of the 1995 Barcelona declaration for its contribution to the development of human resources, specifically in the fields of professional training and educational technologies.

The EAMS mission is to prepare, through education, training and research activities, competent managers from the Arab World and Europe. It develops and promotes, through a collaborative network of partner institutions in both in the Arab World and in Europe, a better understanding of socio-economic and managerial issues that are central to the success of Euro-Arab relations. Most management development programs, on both continents, do not sufficiently address the cultural dimension underlying management concepts and practices. Furthermore, in today's global economy, it is increasingly important for managers to recognize and understand differences in attitudes, values and traditions in their business dealings with others. It is therefore timely and of paramount importance to focus on cross-cultural management and surface-associated issues for study and learning. In addition to disseminating that information to policy-makers and managers through conferences, seminars, workshops and publications, EAMS offers a number of programs.

The Master in Management Development Program (MMDP) trains tutors from EAMS partner institutions, providing skills in bi-cultural (Euro-Arab) management and exposure to new pedagogical developments. The program targets faculty members and trainers who have a degree in management or related fields. Those tutors are used to deliver, within the framework of the Hybrid Business School, a degree program in their home countries which is called the Euro-Arab Management Diploma (EAMD). The approach for the large scale delivery of this EAMD is an interesting example of the concept of the Hybrid Business School. Students from countries such as Italy, Spain, Algeria, Tunisia and Germany have successfully graduated from the program.

The EAMD is offered by the different partner institutions in their respective countries, in collaboration with EAMS, and using the EAMS pedagogical material. It targets managers involved or interested in Euro-

Arab trade, working for any size firm, small to multinationals. The EAMD is a 10-month program.

Since the desired outcome for the manager is to acquire a holistic view of managerial practice, a skills-driven approach is the best way to teach/tutor management at the post-experience level. At the same time, the educational project should ideally fit the personal development path and individual expectations of each student. In practice, it will be more difficult for a Business School to achieve this than for a company, and it is an important change in the pedagogical approach of most Business Schools today. This approach implies a kind of a (moral) learning contract between the student and the Business School that stipulates mutual expectations.

3.1.1.   Learning Strategy

A hybrid learning program should focus on organizational or business processes, analytical, collaborative, contextual, and action mindsets, or be based on a particular in-company project that becomes the backbone of the learning process. In this way, students 'deal' (studies, suggests, compares, etc.) with, for example, the introduction into a new market, a particular possible merger, the implementation of an IT network architecture, and the like. Based on this, a personal learning path can be identified, which includes the study of concepts (out of the pedagogical database), case studies, activities, and workshops. The implementation of a Hybrid Business School program must take into account issues such as accreditation and recognition by the local or international market. Some more work is necessary in order to identify exactly those elements that justify accreditation.

Mass-individualization, in the context of a degree program, can best be realized through a personal learning contract between the learner and the school. An in-company project can be used as an efficient medium for a personal learning contract. The learner enters the course on the condition that he bases this learning on a project that he or she engages in throughout the duration of the course. During this 'learning by doing' phase, a faculty member (facilitator or tutor) guides the learner through the database of material. Those parts of the pedagogical database which form the best input for the project are studied at the particular moment that the learner needs to know the information.

At the same time, the project is the ideal opportunity for the tutor to apply and adapt concepts to local economic and cultural conditions. The project, which is carried out in a particular company in a specific country, is an exercise that relates to local circumstances. The role of the tutor in local adaptation is crucial. The added value of the tutor-based approach, as compared to the open learning approach, is most apparent in the tutor's role in guiding students through their project work.

Whereas the conventional management curriculum is set mainly by fixed academic concerns, the EAMD curriculum is evolutionary in nature and adapted both to business and academic concerns. Hence, the EAMD tries to integrate academic excellence and business relevance in a comprehensive way.

As a result, the EAMD is designed as a self-study, tutor-based management development program. Tutorials are organized and conducted by a local tutors (from the partner institution) who have been trained in Granada on the EAMS 'train-the-trainers program' titled the Master in Management Development Program (MMDP). In addition to tutoring, the EAMD emphasizes the use of actual case studies and project-based or hands-on learning. Often, project-based learning is working on a real project in the organization of the participant, making a direct business contribution and providing an immediate financial return to that organization.

3.1.2. Study Load

The overall workload of the student for the full learning period must be comparable to such a degree elsewhere. The mixture of theory, application and learning by doing should be monitored to be sure it fits within the degree requirements. The pedagogical aim of the course, however, should be to deliver the best possible learning path, enabling the student to fulfil his project and to acquire the necessary knowledge and skills to manage other projects in complex environments in the future.

The EAMD study load consists of course-related work (some self-study and some tutorials) and a project. The course work (to be done in a self-study, tutor-based mode) is based on the bi-cultural, Euro-Arab course material produced by EAMS. It requires approximately 450 hours of self-study time. It is complemented by tutoring sessions of, for instance, three hours once a week over a 10-month period, giving a total of roughly 150 hours. In total, the course work required for the EAMD is equivalent to 600 study hours.

Project work consists of developing an actual case study dealing with a given business situation. The workload for the project/case study is equivalent to 250 hours. This includes all the different stages of the project until the final report is completed. The final report is addressed to the company and presented. The total workload for the EAMD is thus approximately 850 hours.

3.1.3. Admission, Assessment Criteria and Procedures

Each applicant fills out an application form (with enclosures) which can be obtained from the EAMS partner institution in his/her country. Upon return of the completed application, the partner institution makes an evaluation of the candidate's credentials and decides whether or not to invite the candidate to take the Euro-Arab Management Diploma Admission Test (EAMDAT). This test is administered in the different countries of the partner institutions, but processed by EAMS in Granada.

To be admitted onto the EAMD program, a candidate must meet the following criteria:
- Hold an undergraduate university degree;
- Have had a minimum of 2 years of work experience;
- Proficiency in English;
- Succeed the EAMD Admission Test (EAMDAT). (Comparable to the GMAT test, but with less cultural bias.)

Candidates not holding an undergraduate degree may, in exceptional circumstances, be accepted into the EAMD program. The final admission decision is made by EAMS, based on the candidate's score in the EAMDAT test and on his/her application file.

Final assessment of the participant's performance and the awarding of the EAMD is coordinated and administered by EAMS.

3.1.4. Program Design and Content Dimension

In order to give the reader a concrete illustration, figure 6-4 depicts the construction of a possible 'learning route,' navigating the student throughout the pedagogical database. Let's assume that the subject of this route concerns organizational culture, which is a given starting point for the student. From there, individual students can choose their way. All the possible connections (the mentioned concepts, cases and activities) are indicated and reachable by a simple hypertext link. Hence, each student decides what other (related) concepts, cases and activities are of his particular interest. The student designs his learning path in full freedom and according to his needs, knowledge base and learning style.

Figure 6-4 suggests only one possible path. In the case of continuous learning (corporate education), the student can practice much more flexibility as to what, and in what order, he learns, and the degrees of freedom for the student increase.

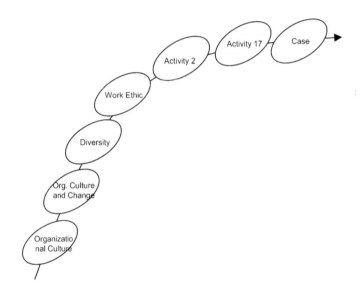

Figure 6-4. Example of a possible learning path

For instance, the student starts reading the concept on organizational culture. In that concept a number of hypertext links exist. S/he chooses to learn more about organizational culture and change. In the latter concept, again a number of hypertext links exist, each time referring to concepts, cases and activities. The student chooses now to learn more about diversity. Clicking on the link, the student is directed to that concept. From there, the student chooses to explore the concept work ethic. In order to illustrate this concept, s/he chooses to try and apply the concept in a particular activity/exercise and therefore clicks on activity 2. Activity 2 gives a short example of how companies manage diverse work ethics, and asks the student to make a short memo on how this concept is dealt with in his/ her company. The student then consults activity 17, which gives a short example on employment policies, taken out of a newspaper report, which the student again relates to his/ her own situation. The student may have become interested in the concept of corporate culture while doing activity 17. S/he may then go to a suggested case on how three companies implemented and manage their organizational cultures.

3.1.5. Delivery Dimension

Since the EAMD has been based on the travelling and growing metaphors of education and learning, many EAMS business school partners need to shift from the subject-centered paradigm to the learner-centered paradigm. This learning philosophy is characterized in a number of different ways. The EAMD attempts to broaden rather than deepen knowledge. The program provides as much flexibility as possible in terms of time and content. Attention is given to developing managerial skills particularly during sit-in sessions such as tutorials. The EAMD is project-based, not only for the above-stated reasons, but also in order to simultaneously create new pedagogical material, and new case material. Self-learning is an integral part of the EAMD program, especially important given the need for flexibility and the time constraints of practicing managers. The idea behind the EAMD is not to train a chosen few, but rather to organize its training programs so as to be able to reach as many people as possible. The local (corporate) cultural component should be present in the EAMD. The tutor plays a crucial role in adapting any pedagogical material to local conditions, whether this means by company or by country. No approach will ever be able to produce pedagogical material to accommodate all particular companies nor all departments inside companies. Local adaptation must thus take place during the tutorials.

The process of material development has involved deconstructing the pedagogical material from its classical textbook format and isolating three categories:

- Concept/ principle library (contextualized definitions with applications);
- Case/ illustration library (case-studies and more extensive examples/ stories);
- Activity learning set (with or without short examples).

Figure 6-5 depicts the case of EAMS and that of its EAMD. Although the initial target was to launch a diploma, EAMS's ultimate aim is to deliver any possible course relevant to management of a particular company and/or country. There is an interesting demand from companies not so much for degree courses at present, but rather for short, specific courses such as finance for engineers, or telecom in the Maghreb countries. With the pedagogical material presented in the form of an electronic database, partners can download the material they need specifically for any particular course. Once the hypertext database is complete, it is very easy to access pedagogical material in order to create specific and specialized degree courses.

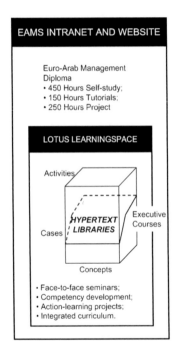

LEARNING ENVIRONMENT

- Internet;
- CD Rom;
- Learning laboratory;
- Communities-of-practice;
- Books

Figure 6-5. The Concept of a Hybrid Business School applied to EAMS

EAMS has chosen Lotus Learning Space as the ICT environment to support its pedagogical material. In addition to the hypertext database, the Lotus Learning Space software offers other advantages that will increasingly become important as the relevant technology is developed and made widely accessible.

The Lotus Learning Space software offers:

- A schedule (guidelines, monitoring)
- A media center or resources with hypertext links to:

-Managerial concepts (independent from functional areas);
-Case-studies and applications;
-Managerial skills or competencies;
- A course room for discussions;
- Profiles (identity of participants in order to facilitate the formation of networks or communities).

The pedagogical material is developed in an electronic format. If participants prefer a paper-based format or if local circumstances dictate the need for it, a paper-based format can be produced based on the electronic format.

For tutors this means that the more flexible the format, the bigger the choice of course material there will be. Tutors become able to tailor programs to the needs of each individual.

Tutors play an important role in adapting any pedagogical material to the local circumstances when necessary. It is unrealistic to think that EAMS could produce material that is country-specific for all of its clients. Thus, the pedagogical material should be ready for use in a "general denominator case." In each particular circumstance, however, it is certain that some cases or even concepts would not apply, or some concepts may apply differently. It is not the role of the tutor to write specific pedagogical material, rather, to organize tutorials per target group.

3.2. The Master Program in Business Innovation & Intrapreneurship of Nyenrode University, the Netherlands Business School

The same concepts previously described and illustrated were also applied in the design and development of the Master in Business Innovation & Intrapreneurship program at Nyenrode University. Nyenrode University is a well-known top-tier graduate business school in the Netherlands. Established in 1946 by large Dutch multinationals such as Shell, Philips and Unilever, Nyenrode, initially set about developing the management skills necessary for the task of rebuilding The Netherlands after the war. Today, Nyenrode University caters the international business community with full-time and part-time business degrees at all levels in addition to academic research.

The management of innovation is perhaps the most challenging task that many organizations face today. Change and innovation have become the norm, not the exception, as argued before. That should equally be reflected in the curriculum of modern day business schools. Thus, the effective management of change and innovation is a major component of Nyenrode's programs.

It is against this background that Nyenrode University offers the Master in Business Innovation & Intrapreneurship (MBI&I) Program, aimed at enabling globally minded business people to perform in an international innovative business world. This program focuses on fostering innovation, while at the same time developing an intrapreneurial spirit within a flexible learning-by-doing academic program, supported with a hybrid learning environment.

For too long, innovation and intrapreneurship have been considered as separate disciplines that could in some way contribute to company's result. The development of the knowledge economy, supported by the existence and increasing use of electronic communication, puts innovation and new idea generation in the fast lane.

Research in innovation suggests that new and innovative ideas are brought to the market mainly by small and new enterprises, rather than by large companies. Particularly under fast changing economic conditions, large companies equally need that very entrepreneurial spirit to turn new ideas into successful products. The competencies that new venturing companies seem to embody as a given are what larger companies would like to acquire and develop. Given the present economic turmoil, the capacity to innovate and "intra-preneur" becomes for most companies more important than ever before. The fact that companies increasingly operate in a networked society requires an additional set of specific managerial competencies.

As we showed earlier, the continuously changing business environment requires managers to comprehend more complex and complicated business dynamics. Creativity, passion, commitment, inspiration, networking, entrepreneurship and leadership are only some competencies that might foster successful development. The MBI&I program aims to develop innovative and entrepreneurial professionals by offering a virtual space where learning takes place and initiative is appreciated. It targets people that have an active role or are appointed to an active role in innovation management. Personal coaching, learning-by-doing projects and workshops cater to the important aspect of 'learning-from-experience.'

The program is centered around a learning laboratory that offers conceptual content, cases, an electronic incubator (which will be illustrated later on), Gartner Business Information services, electronic libraries, and collaborative tools. The content is hypertext-linked, allowing complete freedom of learning at any level of pre-knowledge. The pedagogical concept of learning-by-doing and learning-while-doing, on which the learning lab is based, is the one developed in this book.

The objectives of the MBI&I program are to:
- Introduce employees of companies to intrapreneurial and innovative managerial competencies;
- Provide a higher "return on education" through an immediate and relevant project based learning-by-doing approach;
- Allow for truly international group work and learning, using a hybrid learning laboratory;
- Assist in nurturing innovation in companies, contributing to organizational development;
- Create a network of people and ideas, that are able to generate new business proposals, fostering intrapreneurship inside companies;
- Contribute to personal development of students with an optimal return for the company;
- Deliver high-quality, accredited education;
- Offer truly international business education, with the possibility for the modules to be organized in different locations and different languages.

The program combines projects, virtual (tutor-supported) individual and group studies, and "on-campus face-to-face modules."

3.2.1.   The program format and work load

Over a period of 18 months, 1900 hours of work need to be produced in the following way:

Two intrapreneurial projects, in teams of four or five people, whose goal is to research a real life problem of one of the participating companies. Each project group is assisted by a tutor, who monitors the progress of the group while coaching and supporting them. The project should bring an idea, presented by one of the participants, to a viable, detailed, executable proposal for the development (or production if appropriate) of a particular service or product prepared for a board's decision. A "road book" to assist the students in the discovery of their own innovative approach is available. The outcome of these projects leads to the design and development of one's own innovation approach that can be tested in a protected learning environment. The workload per person for each project is estimated to be 200 hours.

Using the Electronic Incubator, each group is now going to develop a fully new entrepreneurship project. Though the essential difference between this project and the previous ones is the exclusive orientation of the latter on intellectual assets, it clearly makes an allusion to e-business practices. It allows students, for example, to experiment with aspects of the start-up of a new e-business company. Here, students are supported by an e-incubator, a program supporting and guiding them through their endeavor. It also provides the necessary software education and tools in order to realize a concrete e-commerce web site as the project also includes a business plan, as well as the development of a real web site. We will use this e-Incubator further on to illustrate the learning concept of this MBI&I. The time to be allocated for this part is 300 hours.

900 hours of tutor-based self-study, using the Nyenrode Learning Lab. The tentative list of subjects tackled (via assignments and learning-by-doing) is:
- ICT developments;
- Evaluation of intellectual assets;
- Legal aspects of the new economy;
- Cyber marketing;
- Sustainable business and ethics in a networked society;
- Project management;
- Process modeling;
- Multi-cultural cooperative working;
- Self-Organization of Personal Development.

6 one-week on-campus modules spread over the entire 18 months, and another 300 hours of workshops. These workshops aim at confronting students with the latest ideas on any aspect that might be of importance for innovation and intrapreneurship. Workshops can be delivered by both academics and professionals who are known to have challenging ideas or experiences, and can hence contribute to the creative process during this program.

18-MONTHS PERIOD

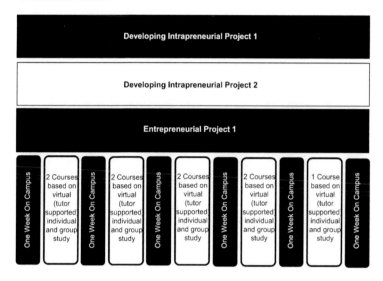

- 700 HOURS PROJECT WORKLOAD;
- 900 HOURS VIRTUAL STUDY LOAD;
- 300 HOURS ON-CAMPUS WORKSHOPS

Figure 6-6. The Structure of the Nyenrode MBI&I

Possible workshops include:

- Learning and the pedagogical concept: the practice of e-learning;
- Does quantifying helps management?
- Post-modern views on management;
- Coaching and its applications;
- Competing with creativity;
- Vision development;
- Does the new economy exist?
- Complexity theory and knowledge;
- Third generation innovation;
- Sustainable business and ethics in a networked society;
- Innovation and renewal management;
- Leadership development as an innovation tool;
- Human Capital;
- Soft Systems Methodology as an action research intervention technique.

3.2.2. The role of faculty

There are five roles that "faculty" can play in this program, quite different from those known in traditional educational programs. For some roles, professionals rather than academics are included.

The *'learning tutor'* co-owns the process of learning. It should again be emphasized that the learner him or herself does remain ultimately responsible for his or her learning and different from classical programs, that responsibility cannot be projected on the tutors (or in a classical program the faculty). A 'learning tutor' supports the students with the subject matters, or what we would call classically the "courses." Since the learning modules are completely self-contained, the role of the tutors is to guide and control the progress of the learner, to point him or her to possible experts that might contribute further, to facilitate the learner's use of the learning lab, or to support in any possible way the student's pedagogical process. Learning tutors are most commonly people with a pedagogical background, trained in supporting electronic learning environments, and who are somewhat familiar with the subject matter. They don't have specific content expertise.

'Project tutors' are equally process owners. Their role is comparable to the learning tutor, but instead of tutoring the "courses" they have a tutor role specifically for the projects mentioned earlier. They also monitor and support the learning process around the projects and support a timely delivery of the required output. The background of the project tutors is based on their experience as entrepreneurs. Ideally, they have gone through this creative and innovative process themselves. Not only can they convey some of their expertise to the students, but more importantly, are able to support the student in the discovery of their own 'best' innovative approach.

The *'content developer'* is probably closest to what we traditionally know as faculty or the teacher. The content developer's role is, in close cooperation with pedagogues, to develop the assignments and concepts. Since no teaching in the traditional sense takes place, it is often pedagogues who draw on expert knowledge in order to develop the course or the pedagogical material. Content developers are also included in order to assess students in specific subject matter. Occasionally, students can be put in contact with these experts if so needed. The background of these content developers is clearly an academic one.

'Workshop facilitators' are also expert owners in addition to challenging advanced and experienced students in their thinking and development.

Workshops can be compared with the better executive education seminars. In most cases, workshop facilitators possess a unique combination of knowledge and expertise, making them an important resource to the student's learning.

Finally, and equally important throughout the entire learning process, are the *'personal development coaches.'* As we indicated earlier, managers have to have the mindset and continuous discipline for personal development, and managing oneself as well as members of the surrounding network. Once the program has finished, the student should possess that competence. This personal development program runs as a red line throughout the program.

3.2.3. Admission and assessment

Candidates should have the following qualifications:
- An educational level equivalent to a Bachelors or Masters degree in Business;
- Approximately 7 to 8 years of experience;
- Sufficient maturity to deal with uncertainty and innovation;
- Experience in learning-by-doing and peer-learning are appreciated;
- The ability to take final responsibility for one's own learning;

An interview with the program director is part of the selection procedure.

Assessment is done by a number of means. Each student has to submit three full reports. Those project reports will then be defended before a jury. A formal exam, oral or written, is used to assess the virtual study modules. Workshops are not graded. Having completed the course work or the workshops with satisfactory results, can lead to a Certificate of Business Innovation and Intrapreneurship. The successful completion of both the virtual course work and the workshops leads to a Diploma in Business Innovation and Intrapreneurship, whereas successful completion of all three parts makes the candidate eligible for a Masters degree.

4. A BRIEF COMPARISON WITH DISTANCE-LEARNING OR TEACHER-CENTERED VIRTUAL MBA'S

The program we just described is based on the Hybrid Business School principles and pedagogical philosophy. Its curriculum attempts to integrate cognitive aspects with creativity and inspirational tools and development, in order to allow managers to create, manage, and operate innovatively within a network of people and companies, according to the current business environment.

What in all this is comparable to distance learning or teacher centered MBAs ?

If one compares this program with the more traditional MBA programs, a number of similarities can be observed. Both program types deliver a degree and are therefore organized according to accreditation requirements. Such accreditation requirements somewhat limit the complete free learning that is striven for in the MBI&I. In practice that means that both program types contain identifiable 'courses' and subject matter.

Both types of programs can also use ICT, though the traditional programs will rather use ICT for supporting the delivery of its program rather than for co-learning and exploration like done in the MBI&I. However, both programs will probably use web site environments as interfaces.

There might be other similarities, such as the ability for students to enter a their convenience, the use of tutors (albeit in different roles as we explained), etc.

What is clearly different then?

A first difference is the starting point. Traditional programs presume that knowledge is transferable, hence, knowledge can be thought. The MBI&I's *pedagogical philosophy* is one where the learner is responsible for his or her learning. As a consequence, traditional programs focus heavily on the content of the learning environment, whereas the MBI&I focuses on the context and on supporting the learning process (for which other technologies are used).

Whereas traditional programs will focus on individual study complemented with group assignments, the MBI&I aims at collaboration and co-learning while improving and changing behavior, rather than just acquiring new knowledge. The latter is only a vehicle in order to acquire the former. This offers a process focus rather than a content drive in the more traditional program types.

Commercially, traditional distance learning approaches, particularly if they are ICT supported, can successfully be made into mass products or commodities. The teacher focus and content approach make them controllable and easy to manage. The process focus of the MBI&I easily allows tailoring, even on an individual level, but as a consequence can be turned into a mass product to less extent.

The *pedagogical approach* of the two types of programs is quite different. As advocated in detail in this book, the MBI&I student is able to decide his or her ideal learning path completely free. Furthermore, all learning takes place via learning-by-doing, either using projects or assignments. Indeed, the MBI&I is definitely a learner-centered, constructivist pedagogical construct whereas the more traditional types of programs remain heavily teacher- and content-centered. As a consequence, they cannot anticipate individual difference in learning needs, style and approach that well as they only support their own pre-defined program structure.

The assessment in each type of programs is different. Due to the choices made and discussed earlier, the MBI&I attempts to assess on the acquired competencies (to deliver output), rather than on the acquired knowledge.

4.1.   An example of a learning path

Bearing in mind the limitations of a static representation of a dynamic process, we would like to briefly illustrate with some screen shots a possible case of the process described in figure 6-7. This outcome shown portrays the learning process that takes place in the student's mind.

The aim of the e-Incubator is to support the teams to develop their own e-commerce, in basically two steps: first to develop a business plan; then to design and build a web site. The e-Incubator structures this learning process somewhat, provides additional information and exercises if the student requires them, delivers a template for the business plan, and has at any stage hypertext links to relevant content of the learning lab. The business plan template is co-developed within the project group, employing the collaborative tools of the learning lab. In the learning process, each individual can choose his or her own learning path. During the assignment, collaboration is necessary.

Figure 6-7 illustrates a sequence the student chose. We will later discuss each of those screens separately. The left column of the screen provides the navigation through the e-Incubator, the right part of the screen depicts the content. On top of the screen some buttons allow general navigation through the whole learning lab. Colored words indicate hypertext links.

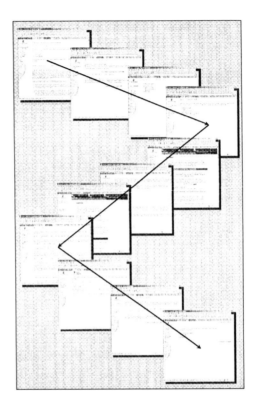

Figure 6-7

The sequence is the following:
- On the start screen the student for the example of the business plan (that s/he can read on screen, which is not printed here);
- Then the learner decides to explore some of the key topics of such a business plan;
- S/he explores the header Target Market & Positioning;
- The learner decides to learn more about segmentation;
- While doing that, s/he contemplates that s/he doesn't know what target markets are, and hence explores that concept (further exploring more concepts, that are not illustrated here);
- (the possibility to go back to the template, whenever ready, in order to start working on the business plan is not illustrated here)
- The student wants to start building the web site;

- S/he finds our what needs to be done;
- The learner explores application design (and could download the necessary software for doing so, which is not printed here);
- (After a few more steps, not illustrated here) the student decides to start building his/ her web site and can choose a number of software products to download in order to do so.

Let us now have a brief look on the different individual screens.

The first screen is the starting screen of the e-Incubator. Both in the left-hand column and in the main area, one can click the three subdivisions of the e-Incubator: the business plan; the design of the site; and the soft-launch. In the learning path that we illustrate here, the student clicks on the left hand side on "Example and template," which is one of the two sub-headings under 'Business Plan.' Throughout the work in the e-Incubator, the student keeps the same 'look-and-feel,' as well as the same navigational possibilities. As already indicated earlier, but made more clear here, the top navigation bar allows the user to return to the learning lab.

Figure 6-8. e-Incubator starting screen

162

As discussed in chapter 3, lots of ICT tools are available in order to make the user interface as attractive as possible, and to offer some "infotainment" options As one can see from this example, we have chosen not to do so in this program, based on the limited bandwidth that is commonly available. Regardless, the platform allows integration of full multimedia. It is not yet proven, however, as will be discussed later, that more multimedia guarantees better learning results.

Once the student has clicked, s/he comes in the previous screen.

Figure 6-9. e-Incubator screen 2

This screen offers the student the option to either have a look into a real life case, an e-business business plan (in this case of the company called E-Valley), or to request a download of the business plan template. Imagine that the student first has a look into the business plan, in order to get a clue of what is eventually expected. At a later stage, when the student feels comfortable enough to commence writing the business plan for the group assignment, s/he can return to this screen. For the time being, the student chooses to explore a little more about the key topics that should be present in the business plan. For that, s/ he clicks in the left column on "key topics," under the heading "Business plan".

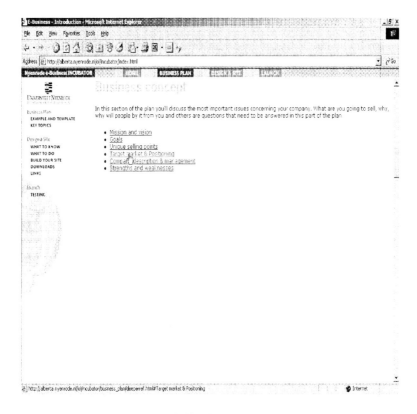

Figure 6-10. e-Incubator screen 3

The business concept screen presents six titles and the student would like to learn more about "Target market & positioning."

A minimal description is offered about what is to be understood under target market and positioning, after which the student could chose to explore any of the elements of this topic in more detail. Depending on how familiar the student feels with the different topics, s/he might prefer to learn more about "Segmentation." At that moment, the e-Incubator "sends" the request to the learning lab, where all the concepts are organized. The next screen that then will be displayed describes the concept "Segmentation" as it is stored in the content database.

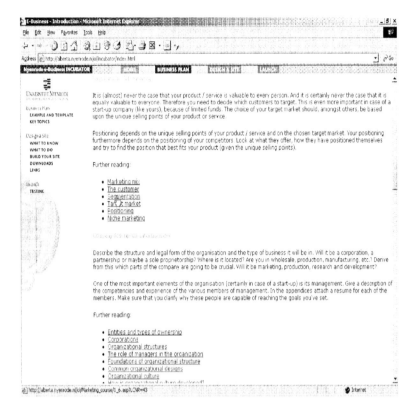

Figure 6-11. e-Incubator screen 4

The student can now read the concept, do possible mini-assignments that are included, look at an attached (example) video if available, or whatever s/he deems necessary for his or her own learning. As one can see, throughout the text some of the concepts are highlighted. That means that there is a hypertext link to that concept and in case the student needs more understanding s/he can click through to that concept. At the end of certain concepts, a list of related concepts is added as well as a related case list. Consequently, the student decides to click on the concept "target markets," since s/he doesn't really understand that issue clearly.

In the next screen, a number of hypertext links are displayed. For the demonstration, we assume that the student now feels s/he has enough background in order to start the assignment - writing the business plan for a new business.

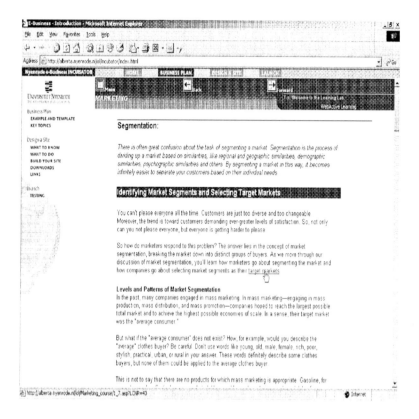

Figure 6-12. e-Incubator screen 5

Hence, using the navigation in the left column, s/he clicks again on an example that will lead the student back to the earlier screen where s/he had the choice between getting an example or downloading the template.

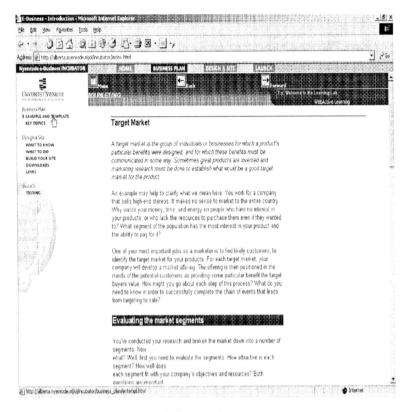

Figure 6-13. e-Incubator screen 6

One can now recognize the same screen as before allowing the student to download the template. The template is exactly the same format as the one used in the Incubator itself which makes it easy for the student to click back to the e-Incubator and/or the learning lab for more content backing at any point in time.

This procedure has demonstrated the first part of the e-Incubator, preparing for the business plan. It equally illustrates both the seamless interaction between e-Incubator and learning lab, and the hypertext links in the learning lab concepts. The combination of seamless connections between assignment and learning lab, and the hypertext organization displayed here, is key in the realization of the pedagogical concept.

Figure 6-14. e-Incubator screen 7

The student now chooses (for this demo) to explore the second part of the e-Incubator, related to effectively building a web site. On the previous screen it can be seen that s/he has chosen to click in the navigation of the left column, the subheading "what to do" under the chapter on the "design of the site." One then receives the following screen.

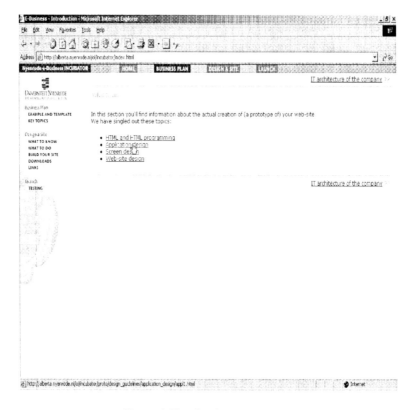

Figure 6-15. e-Incubator screen 8

The student now has the option to choose between learning more about HTML programming; application design; screen design; or web-site design. In this case, the student decides on the application design option, which brings him or her to the next screen.

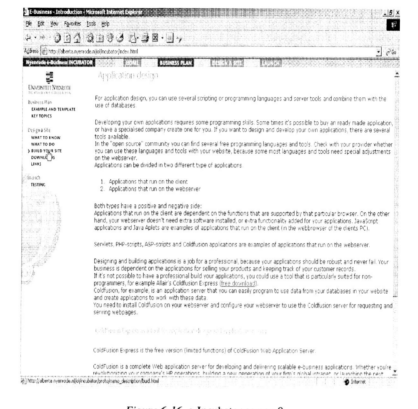

Figure 6-16. e-Incubator screen 9

This screen explains what is meant by application design and what is required. This e-Incubator is not aimed at supporting computer science students who want to learn about application design, but targets managers who most probably have never looked at web design before.

The information, therefore, is detailed, but very much hands-on. Once the student feels familiar with the concept, s/he can download software to effectively help him or her with the application design. If the student would like to see what "Build your site" offers, under the same header of "design of the site" (in the left-hand column), s/ he can click that topic.

Figure 6-17. e-Incubator screen 10

The student now has the choice of a number of software tools in order to effectively build a web site. At this stage, the student is expected to have completed an application and screen design, using earlier parts of the e-Incubator. The remainder of the assignment consists of building the web site based on the different designs made. If at this point the learner finds out s/he has missed insight, the left column navigation allows the student to go back and explore (further).

This ends the short demonstration of a possible use of the e-Incubator. The e-Incubator can be considered as one of the many assignments that students need to work on during their study for the MBI&I. Other assignments are structurally no different from this incubator.

REFERENCES

Collins, J. (2001), Good to Great: Why Some Companies Make the Leap... and Others Don't. Harper Collins.

Hamel, G. (2002), Leading the Revolution: How to Thrive in Turbulent Times by Making Innovation a Way of Life. Plume.

Van der Linden, G. and Parker, P. (1999). An Exploration of Paradoxes in Managerial and Organizational Complexity: A Postmodern Interpretation of Corporate Vision. In: Baets, W. (ed.) *Complexity and Management, A Collection of Essays, Vol 1*, World Scientific Publishing: Singapore.

Chapter 7

The Learning Mindset Scan: a Methodology for Developing Corporate Learning Ventures

1. IMPLEMENTING COMBINED ORGANIZATIONAL AND INDIVIDUAL LEARNING

As we stressed earlier, the knowledge-creating and learning organization perspectives bring about a strong and complex process that has an important impact on every aspect of the organization and its members. Knowledge and learning touch all of the assumptions underlying the organization's structures and processes, and changes the roles, responsibilities, competencies and activities of all involved.

Organizational learning magnifies and closes the loop of individual learning within a dynamic corporate and networked setting that allows the learning process inside a company to excel beyond efficiency frontiers. The organization's strategies and capabilities - everything from resources, (infra)-structures and support systems to enabling constraints and core philosophy - will drive that organizational learning. But individual learning is exactly based on those elements - contextualized - as well as individualized, based on individual roles, needs, and learning style. This individual learning then is to be complemented with shared experimentation and application. We refer to the flow from learning platform to collaborative learning lab and knowledge tank whereby new knowledge is created in a collaborative environment. The combination and flow between all of these elements closes and magnifies the loop of organizational learning, thus describing the tension and interaction between individual learning and organizational learning. It also portrays all the concrete aspects of the Hybrid Business School concept, namely the blended platform with its specific philosophy, the learning lab and knowledge tank, and the two methodologies that we want to discuss further in this chapter.

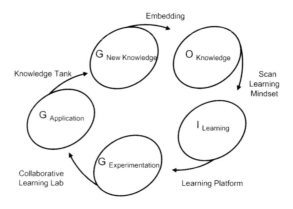

Figure 7-1. The elements that make a complete learning venture

In order to maximize the potential of the Hybrid Business School project, and to unearth tangible and authentic individual and business benefits, a swift and transparent methodology is required to assist organizations and institutions in defining and creating the appropriate learning and knowledge management environment. This methodology, called "Learning Mindset Scan," is instrumental in making such learning projects concrete and manageable, and should therefore identify and build on the organization's specific situation, learning needs and culture, and the appropriate technological solutions. The Learning Mindset Scan methodology offers companies a complete business case for learning and knowledge, including the needed investment and ROI, hence the use of the word venture. The "Embedding" methodology then describes the integration of the technological solution and output of the knowledge tank and learning lab with the organization's strategy, processes, and procedures, and the complete implementation of the Hybrid Business School concept within its specific situation.

Besides the need to increase and develop their human capital and manage corporate knowledge, companies can find themselves in situations where a learning venture based on the Hybrid Business School concept delivers additional business benefits beyond performance. Change and turnaround processes, the redirection or implementation of long-term vision and strategy, vertical or horizontal integration through mergers and acquisitions, high dependency on R&D and innovation, decentralizations and de-mergers, spin-offs and spinouts, and high growth are among the angles where a learning venture offers tangible added value.

Learning institutions also have to carefully consider their specific situation and environment in order to develop a degree program. Issues such as target audience and the role they might play within a corporate environment, the ambitions towards providing life-long and continuous learning, including knowledge domains, should be taken into consideration.

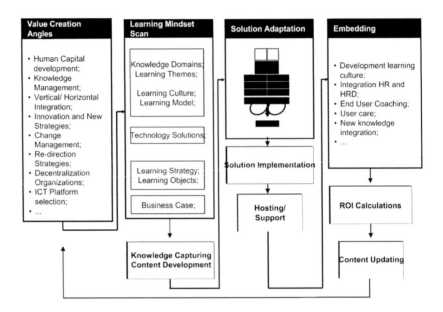

Figure 7-2. Learning Mindset and Embedding Methodologies

2. ENABLING CONSTRAINTS FOR LEARNING VENTURES

Before dealing with a concrete methodology, we must highlight some important boundary conditions and enabling constraints for learning ventures. One of the most important key success factors in the development of a learning center or corporate university is the continuous and active support of top (and senior) management. They shape the learning culture and knowledge management approach of the organization; they are its ambassadors. If topmanagement is unable to create a learning environment that allows and supports continuous (online) learning, then the Hybrid Business School approach will remain a project with limited success. This learning environment is the necessary and important link between the corporate strategy and the changing role of management as depicted in chapter 1. Senior management plays a key role in acting as a catalyst for creating such a learning environment. Senior management must advise and allow personnel to take part in management development activities of any kind. The learning environment must be supported by a defined internal and external communication strategy. It is important to continuously communicate the links among the strategy, HR development, training, knowledge management, and the learning platform. If this communication does not exist in a company, external help should be contracted. Given the financial value of the investment in this learning approach, internal branding is an important issue.

A second prerequisite is that line management also needs to support the learning approach. They must create a culture of learning, which is translated into the daily practice of each employee. Of course, job evaluations should focus on developmental issues, and it should be easy for the learner to apply what s/he learns. The learner also should be enabled to make the translation between what is learned and the daily practice or application.

These boundary conditions might not sound new or even important, as it is generally understood that the support of line and senior management is vital to the learning process. In our experience, however, we have seen too many cases in which support existed on paper, and not in practice. In too many cases, management doesn't see development as a valuable management practice that they should actively steer and support. There are numerous cases in which line management wasn't given the tools to support their staff in their development endeavor, senior management lost interest after a couple of months ("it looks nice for internal and external PR when we do this"), and colleagues were not to transfer any learning.

Last, appointing an "independent" program coordinator could be beneficial in the development of a successful learning venture. Possibly, this could be an external (interim) manager. The coordinator needs to have the knowledge and experience about the pedagogical and methodological approach as s/he plays the role of liaison between the participants (the learners), the educational providers (institutions and their staff/faculty/tutors), and the firm (HRD and HR management, and senior executives). Being external to the company, s/ he can assure that liaison role without bias or specific role. The coordinator must also brief faculty about the company and its specific issues, the participants, the learning project, the contribution of individual faculty members for the learning project (also to create synergies), corporate and individual development paths, and assess the overall quality.

The coordinator is often involved from the onset in the development of the venture, the identification, choice and selection of the educational partners and/or faculty. S/he has an overall coaching role with the participants. Hence, the coordinator also has to have the necessary academic credibility combined with corporate credibility and an expertise of organizational and strategic analysis as well as management processes.

3. THE LEARNING MINDSET SCAN

We will now give an overview of the whole Learning Mindset Scan, comprising of the identification of knowledge domains and learning themes, learning culture and learning model, ICT solutions, overall learning strategy and learning objects, and the business case, before starting knowledge capturing and content development.

3.1. Knowledge domains and learning themes

Most visions are a muddled stew of values, goals, purposes, philosophies, beliefs, aspirations, norms, strategies, practices, and descriptions while most strategic implementation plans involve dense documents filled with numbers and jargon. Building the process of understanding an organization around a strategic picture or profile yields much better results. We break down the strategic profile into strategic resources, innovation and growth, customer value, and financials before translating them into learning themes and knowledge domains.

Strategic resources include core competencies, strategic assets, and core processes, and the unique way in which they are combined, and exploited in a distinctly competitive way. A core competency is the firm's knowledge, encompassing skills and unique capabilities, whereas strategic assets encompass brands, patents, infrastructure, customer data, and anything that is both rare and valuable. Core processes are methodologies, activities and routines used in transforming inputs into outputs. They are used in translating competencies, assets, and other inputs into value for customers.

Innovation and growth refers to the organization's value network as well as disruptive and sustaining innovation DNAs. The value network clearly complements and amplifies the firm's resources. Its elements include suppliers, partners, alliances, and coalitions. Disruptive innovations signal their arrival long before they bloom while sustaining innovations refer to new products or processes developed on the shop or office floor. With the innovation DNA aspect, we refer to the way an organization has installed processes and policies to drive or increase such innovations. Both these innovation DNAs will also give us a first indication of the inherent organizational learning capacity.

We then plot the customer value: customer relationship, brand identity, and the performance of the product or service offering and its delivery relative to other alternatives along the key success factors that define competition in the industry or category. First, the plot shows the strategic profile of an industry by depicting clearly the factors that affect competition among industry players, as well as those that might in the future. Second, it shows the strategic profile of current and potential competitors, identifying which factors they invest in strategically. Last, it further draws the company's strategic profile showing how it invests in the factors of competition and delivering customer value, and how it might invest in them in the future.

In order to complete this picture, we look into financial processes such as to how revenue is created (the business model) and how productivity growth is cultivated.

The strategic picture derived from this exercise actually records the company's customer capital, organizational capital, partner capital, and environmental capital, the result of which then can be filtered down to the level of specific roles, including role and competency profiles, and required human capital within the organization. Combined with a gap analysis between future requirements, current requirements, and the present situation, it offers us an indication not only of what knowledge domains and themes are crucial for the organization, but also the internal and external needs in terms of learning and knowledge.

3.2. Learning culture and learning model

A corporation cannot go through any process of designing a learning venture without investigating its culture and guiding principles. The corporate culture will mainly guide the learning culture and the vision on learning and sharing knowledge. Reflecting a statement of who they are, what they stand for, what they are about, barriers and restrictive boundary conditions as described above are mostly hidden in the organization's culture.

We can understand the corporate culture through its core values and core purpose, and how they are realized and made tangible. It exists as an internal element, not determined by the (prevailing) state of the environment. Core values refer to the firm's essential and enduring tenets. They are a small set of general guiding principles not to be confused with the specific cultural or operational practices, or to be compromised for financial gain or short-term expediency. The core purpose describes the organization's fundamental reason for existence beyond just making money - a perpetual guiding star on the horizon, not to be confused with specific goals or business strategies. The social contract, design of the physical space, organizational structure, leadership style, social relationships, business conduct, symbols and rituals, are among the elements through which we can analyze the culture.

Based on such analysis, the appropriate learning culture and the exact learning (pedagogical) model can then be defined. An important aspect of learning culture is the acknowledgement and acceptance that employees can fail in their roles and that one can learn a lot from failure - provided that one encourages people to share their experiences in this respect. Members of a learning community should receive moral and emotional support for learning. A learning community is a vehicle for sharing experiences, information, ideas, and knowledge, for developing an insight into patterns, where resources and intellectual technologies are combined. Within this learning community, members participate as partners in a joint undertaking to advance learning and therein shape educational provision. Further, it is crucial for learning and knowledge management to be harmonized. Learning can be seen as an important vehicle in developing "emergent" strategies, and managing knowledge as well as the organization's capabilities that trigger organizational learning. In this, technology is considered to be an enabler that accelerates learning within the organization. Last, the learning culture will also reflect on the communication and internal marketing as well as the professional image of the venture.

The learning model will then include all pedagogical concerns described in chapters 5 and 6. It aims at delivering individualized learning, based on previous knowledge and experience, present role and specific needs. It also allows for different forms of learning and different aspects of what should be learned. The learning model comprises pedagogical principles on which the learning process will be organized, the instructional method, the role of faculty, processes and procedures, what will be delivered virtually and what not, the didactic approach, media, and the roles of the HR and HRD department vis-à-vis line and senior management. It seems important to point out that we endorse a combination of the 'travelling' and 'growing' pedagogic paradigms. The travelling metaphor advocates a more holistic and self-organizing principle. It is the learner who is in charge and responsible for his or her learning process (self-organized learning). The growing metaphor, then, focuses on personality development.

Some of the following questions might be helpful in deciding the appropriate learning model:

- What are the learning and knowledge-sharing goals of the company? What expectations does the company have of its staff in this respect?
- Can you define how the company will be able to realize these learning objectives?
- How will you harmonize the individual learning objectives so that they are consistent with the goals of the company?
- What experiences of colleagues would you like to be able to consult?
- How would you reward the contribution of individual learning to the corporate knowledge base?
- What is the role of a personal development path?
- What criteria will you use to recruit staff to the company? How will these criteria support the development of the learning culture?
- What mechanisms for information sharing should be introduced to support cross-departmental knowledge sharing?
- What kind of knowledge do you want senior management to share with staff within the company?

3.3.   ICT solution

The right choice of ICT solution is critical in the development of a learning venture. The platform must be instrumental to the knowledge management strategy identified and selected by the company, and should reflect its overall learning culture and learning model. The wrong choice of platform may well constrain the learning venture's development, implementation, and success.

It would be wrong to choose a platform based on technical considerations only. We have seen that too many organizations see learning and knowledge management purely as an ICT project, only to realize their mistake after the purchase of a particular platform or solution. Very often, that choice doesn't support the required learning model and all of its aspects. At all times, the latter will drive the selection process as technology is considered to be an enabler that accelerates learning and knowledge management within the organization (and not vice versa).

The architecture and infrastructure should easily and at all times be integrated with an organization's (existing) business processes and ICT-infrastructure - applications that might be deemed to add value to the learning process. From this, completely new business functions will evolve and the organization will gain new insights. The learning venture becomes an "initiator of progress," and in true business terms, it magnifies the returns on original investments. Important, however, is that the required functionalities are listed via the "MOSCOW" method (must have, should have, could have, want to have), based on an identification and evaluation of available and selected applications.

As we explained in chapter 5, the Hybrid Business School concept can be built, for the most part, using existing, off the shelf, standard software around a core engine. Each software component is highly advanced and has proven itself under many different circumstances. By using standard or generic software as much as possible, one can take full advantage of the broad range of functionalities and continuous development associated with such software. This lowers any risks involved, lowers the time to implement and lowers the costs of maintenance. The true uniqueness of our proposed technology solution lies, not so much in the individual components but in the way they have been creatively combined and in some cases used in a totally new way. Each firm involved in a learning venture should take that approach, given its specific situation, learning model and learning culture.

If these are the general guidelines by which the platform should be designed, what can we say about the components to be included within the architecture? Clearly, a number of internal and external information (re)sources which will constitute the database framework are to be included. Electronic libraries containing reference material and articles in an electronic, browsable, and searchable format, or general information sources, or databases of partner organizations and alliances can be linked or made accessible. As a consequence, information filtering and dedicated (multimedia) search engines will be central to the effectiveness of the platform. Finally, it might be interesting to link some specific, but more detailed courses (such as web-based courses, or CD-ROMS) that allow students to explore further any particular area of interest.

Collaborative tools, communication technologies, content management, virtual learning technologies, portal management and management reporting solutions, learning management system, and pedagogical technologies represent the main building blocks of the architecture. Other crucial aspects are the user interface and accessibility. At all times, it is the architecture that accommodates the individual and not, as so often can be found, the other way around. Hence the chosen platform should be designed in a way that it allows the organization and delivery of e-learning (and again, we do not mean e-teaching here) in an appropriate way, given the specifics of the environment and target audience.

The selected components, modalities, and functionalities are to be linked around the Hybrid Business School core engine. This engine guarantees nonlinear dynamic and flexible, contextualized and individualized learning through its matching function. As previously described, an individual learner's curriculum based on previous knowledge and experience, and present job function and roles, is created dynamically and automatically structured and delivered as learning content, in the appropriate form, to the learner. The learner then defines what is "appropriate," when, and how it is appropriate (learning style). The learner's performance and progress are then continuously assessed and tracked, the results are processed and weighed, after which they are matched with the learner's profile. The combination of Case Based Reasoning Systems, expert systems, intelligent agents, and Artificial Neural Networks is a strong backbone for the knowledge and learning network we envision.

3.4.   Overall learning strategy and learning objects

Content and delivery merge in the Hybrid Business School's overall learning strategy. The merger brings together the analysis made on the level of knowledge domains and learning themes, the learning culture and learning model chosen, and the possibilities of the ICT solutions selected.

Central to the overall learning strategy is the integrated curriculum that focuses on business, organizational, managerial, and strategic processes. Management, however, is not to be understood as the equation of different disciplines. Education should not be based on functions but on roles, activities, and questions. In other words, the learning strategy refers to complete development paths and learning agendas as required within a particular organization's environment. The learning agenda, the "courses," are nothing more than a learning-by-doing agenda, as described earlier. The learning agenda includes the individual learning cycles, the collaborative learning space (consisting of a learning laboratory or collaborative forum, and communities-of-practice, and the Knowledge Tank), the peer-to-peer, issue-driven, blended platform aimed at establishing a continuous knowledge-creating process. The knowledge-creating process is driven by interest groups (knowledge spaces) that focus on a limited number of new issues, concepts, and challenges.

Based on this learning strategy, learning objects now have to be defined. The pedagogical material is organized differently than the traditional functional textbook format in order to accommodate the hypertext platform. It is not the electronic form that alters the delivery, but it also reflects the overall learning strategy depicted earlier. Subject matters are seen as a set of experiences each student should absorb. Learning objects are defined in four different segments.

Concepts represent selected pieces of theory on a specific aspect of management. These concepts will be hypertext-linked (in addition to the other segments). This means that if one comes across a link to a related concept in the text, then that new concept is only a click away. Based on this approach, learning pathways no longer need to be prescribed; any user may learn how s/he wants. The learner can explore as much as s/ he desires.

Cases and stories (narratives) are illustrations of how a number of concepts are used in practice. They will also be hypertext-linked with the other segments.

Together with the best practices or guiding principles, they represent the accumulated corporate learning and experiences. Obviously, those best practices and guiding principles should be related to concepts. Similarly, concepts are more insightful when they relate to illustrations of the theory they are covering. A broad integration of concepts and their mutual interdependencies is more important than a deep understanding of any particular concept.

Last, managerial competencies reflect the particularities of managerial roles. Competency development in terms of generic, organic and changing competencies as described earlier, reflect the capacity of creating new businesses and strategic resources, technologies and capabilities, and products and services. Repositories of such competencies associated with concepts, narratives, and best practices are to be defined, more importantly because managerial competencies are sustained by continuous learning.

This brings us to our element of activity learning in which learning is put into practice. Within the hypertext platform, this segment directs us to tools and solutions in which the student will be actively involved, and ranging from simulations, templates, to problem solving tasks. Within the Hybrid Business School, learning is driven via a learning agenda, a set of activities that need to be completed, i.e. a learning-by-doing approach. Since each user decides on a path that s/he wishes to follow based on individual needs, learning does not take place via a fixed learning path but rather via a coordinated and agreed set of targets to reach. Learners are helped in this process by the set of activities, which are designed to direct learners through the relevant concepts and cases. The more concepts, cases and activities are interlinked, the richer the database becomes and the more possible learning paths can be created. Consequently, relevant experience is necessary to construct such activities. The quality of these activities is of paramount importance for the success of the learning venture and hence requires a lot of effort.

Universities and learning institutions traditionally position education at a theoretical level, mainly via concepts and some cases. Companies however, will always be more interested in the application of learning. Often, these two views of learning do not complement each other. In the Hybrid Business School we make it a priority that they do through its J-learning (just in time, just appropriate, just enough) approach.

Faculty plays a crucial role in the success of the Hybrid Business School, as they have to shift their pedagogical approach and their practical involvement radically. Faculty, subject specialists, and guest speakers need thorough explanation, likely training or retraining to learn how to become tutors, mentors and guides, rather than teachers, and thoroughly understand the pedagogical concept of the Hybrid Business School. The project and activity focus is another area where faculty may need coaching.

The personal development evaluation should monitor the follow up process of the course delivery and the learning on the level of each individual employee. While the ideal is to plug in the learning process in the personal development trajectory of the participants, other forms of evaluation could be used. In some cases (for instance learning projects leading to a company MBA or an accredited degree), it could be advisable to go through a student selection process at the start of the program, using an entry test, an interview, or both. The entry test should focus on the learning attitude and related process variables, rather than simply on standard intellectual performance. It remains, however, a difficult task for a firm to decide on its criteria for selection. The process of enrolment, equally, has to be designed.

We have introduced the use of an intake to draw an individual profile that can be used in the core engine of our concept and solution. Elements such as previous knowledge and experience, the role someone has, the level of complexity he or she can handle, and their competency profile could be recorded and made part of such an individual profile. Once the learner has entered the learning cycle, the learning process then needs to be continuously monitored in view of qualification for diplomas. The focus of measurement, however, switches from 'content and result' to 'learning, improved process and attitude.' A mixture of self-evaluations and evaluations with a tutor could cover that aspect. The content of both the individual profile and the self-evaluation/ evaluation measurement has to be designed. All of this information and results may later feed in to existing HR databases and linked to career planning, performance appraisal information. On the other hand, all of this information can be made part of the individual profile used in the entry test.

The learning venture must then be communicated clearly to potential learners as it is important that their expectations match the philosophy.

3.5. Business case

Before we can start with content development and knowledge capturing, the learning venture's business case has to be completed.

This business case will start off by portraying the company's strategic profile and perspective on learning. Where lies the exact opportunity for learning and knowledge management? What is the delivery in terms of learning culture, learning model, and ICT solution? How will the (internal and/ or external) market be addressed, i.e. its communication and branding?

Obviously, an organizational model, including all (internal and external) partners, suppliers, core team, human resources, and their roles and deliveries, with all the surrounding processes, needs to be drawn up. Detailed roll-out plans with milestones, timings, owners, processes, performance indicators, and the investment case for each of those elements should be outlined. In case of a commercial learning venture, or the positioning of learning and knowledge management as a business center with P/L responsibility, the appropriate business model and revenue streams will be determined.

The clear definition of performance indicators and business benefits alongside strategy is important in order to be able to calculate the return-on-investment. In addition, some methods to calculate a firm's intangible assets or human capital could be used to estimate the learning venture's ROI. In order to get a more dynamic picture of the obtained ROI, such calculations could be repeated in time.

3.6.　Knowledge capturing and content development

Specific, detailed and multimedia content can now be developed. The level of use of multimedia obviously highly depends on the availability of broadband. It is important to first deconstruct themes into questions and activities. This could happen using mind mapping or similar techniques. As the organizing idea behind the content is experience, subject experts and knowledge creators who "know what" and "know how" around particular questions or activities have to be identified and appointed. Those could be in-house experts or experts from an educational partner(s) or publisher(s). They provide the complete context of the content and knowledge they are responsible for, starting with the definition of a list of generic yet context-sensitive questions and activities and the processes of getting to answers. For each of the questions and activities, knowledge and content has to be "tagged" and developed according to the segments described above.

The aim is to store and organize explicit, implicit and learned knowledge within the learning platform. Commonly, making knowledge explicit already exists in companies, covering containing rules, calculation methods, etc. Given that we have selected an open style platform, there should be no problem in connecting those existing company databases. Implicit and learned experiences, however, can best be included in a case-based reasoning system: a kind of a database that contains stories in such a way that they can be structured and reassembled within the environment. Explicit and implicit knowledge should be linked as much as possible by hypertext. This structure allows the learner to explore as much as s/he desires, without having to be knowledgeable about the way the material is structured beforehand.

Based on this, a selection between aggregated content or own company content can be made. At all times, the company should discuss who holds the copyright and also nondisclosure issues have to be researched. In education, we are accustomed to working with books, for which the copyright law is clear. The legal issues concerning copyright on electronic material and copyright on paper-based material used in an electronic environment, however, are still vague. Publishers do not always have a clear-cut policy and are in general reluctant concerning copyright on the electronic use of their pedagogical material. Today, this remains an important concern for the design and implementation of a learning venture.

Subject experts and knowledge creators will provide initial content objects to editors who are responsible for the consistent formatting of content. It is important that each learning object only contains a few text pages, since text longer than a few pages becomes unreadable for most users. Multimedia content not only allows for a higher degree of infotainment, but also enables learners to select the medium that is closest to his or her learning style. Besides the functional design, the technical design needs careful attention. Standards such as AICC and SCORM have to be taken into account where possible.

In addition, it is necessary to create a robust thesaurus of synonyms. This allows the identification of a rich diversity of terms, not necessarily consistent or coordinated in a centrally logical sense, but important to learners. If each learning object has meta-data attached, it will allow further clustering via a relevancy ranking from 1 to 5. This will enable the personalized content generator to learn and select or direct to more relevant learning objects and information resources.

Both the development of more general narratives (based on projects of alumni and students) or the development of new (industry or company specific) cases and illustrations are very important. Narratives need to be understood as a set of pedagogical cases, stories, or life experiences. They are examples and illustrations of applications of concepts in a particular industry, market, or company context. Their role in the pedagogical database is a key connection between knowledge management and virtual learning. The complexity of writing a more process and hypertext based (multimedia) case with clear links to the subject matter database should not be underestimated. The least attractive possibility is using existing teaching cases or otherwise publicly available materials. This approach doesn't fit the Hybrid Business School concept.

Three kinds of information sources need to be added in the wider circle of the pedagogical database. The first extension is to build in access to an electronic library, containing books and journal articles, in an electronic, browsable and searchable format. The second extension is to offer students direct and linked access to general information sources or databases. Finally, it can be interesting to link some very specific, but more detailed courses. An added value of this latter extension is the fact that it helps in the accreditation process in any particular legal framework or country, as in the traditional educational and accreditation system (additional) functional courses are a parameter for recognition. Therefore, the value of the degree and the potential for accreditation increase within more traditional university accreditation systems, as they exist today (e.g. the AACSB and EQUIS/EQUAL accreditations).

3.7.   Embedding

The final phase of our methodology (see figure 4-3) now comprises the complete implementation of the chosen ICT solution and start-up of the learning venture, starting with its adaptation according to the selected functionalities, ICT environment and specificities of the organization and its business environment. The implementation of the solution's hardware and software, and its integration with existing platforms, follows this phase. This is not a sole task for ICT-consultants, as process owners should work with them at all times. Typically, traditional ICT project management methods can be used.

The broader embedding starts with the rollout of the business case (which should be considered as a business or project plan) and all of its aspects. The core team's first concentration should lie the thorough development of the learning culture, and integration within HR and HRD processes and policies. The role of line and senior management then starts. Consequently, the communication strategy has to be brought to life.

Once these aspects have been put to work and have been tested, the selection and enrollment of students can be initiated, followed by a process of end-user coaching (and later on continuous user care). This could be organized via workshops or on a one-to-one basis depending on the number of students enrolled.

Special attention should also go to processes surrounding the reintegration of new knowledge from the collaborative learning space and knowledge tank.

BUILDING BLOCKS OF THE LEARNING MINDSET SCAN AND EMBEDDING METHODOLOGIES

Learning Mindset Scan

- Break down the strategic profile into strategic resources, innovation and growth, customer value, and financials before translating them into learning themes and knowledge domains;
- The strategic picture derived from this exercise actually records the company's customer capital, organizational capital, partner capital, and environmental capital;
- The result can be filtered down to the level of specific roles, including role and competency profiles, and required human capital within the organization, and linked to a gap analysis between future requirements, current requirements, and the present situation;
- A firm cannot go through any process of designing a learning venture without investigating its culture and guiding principles;
- The corporate culture will mainly guide the learning culture and the vision on learning and sharing knowledge;
- The learning model comprises of the pedagogical principles on which the learning process will be organized, the instructional method, the role of faculty, processes and procedures, what will be delivered virtually and what not, the didactic approach, media, and the roles of the HR and HRD department vis-à-vis line and senior management;
- The ICT solution must be instrumental to the knowledge management strategy identified and selected by the company, and should reflect its overall learning culture and learning model;
- Collaborative tools, communication technologies, content management, virtual learning technologies, portal management and management reporting solutions, learning management systems, and pedagogical technologies represent the main building blocks of the architecture. Other crucial aspects are the user interface and accessibility;
- The selected components, modalities, and functionalities are to be linked around the Hybrid Business School core engine;
- Central to the overall learning strategy is the integrated curriculum that focuses on business, organizational, managerial, and strategic processes and refers to complete development paths and learning agendas as required within a particular organization's environment;

The learning agenda and complete development path not only include the individual learning cycles, but also those of the collaborative learning space and the Knowledge Tank;

Based on this learning strategy, learning objects now have to be defined in four different segments, namely concepts, narratives, best practices/ guiding principles, and managerial competencies;

Faculty members have to be trained in their new roles, as they have to shift their pedagogical approach and their practical involvement radically;

The process of enrolment, intake, and personal development assessment have to be designed and criteria selected;

The business case describes all elements of previous analysis, branding and communication, organizational model, detailed roll-out plans, performance indicators and business benefits alongside strategy, appropriate business model and revenue streams, and ROI calculation.

Embedding

Comprises the complete implementation of the chosen ICT solution and start-up of the learning venture, starting with its adaptation according to the selected functionalities, ICT environment and specificities of the organization and its business environment;

Traditional ICT project management methods can be used for the implementation of the solution's hardware and software, and its integration with existing platforms;

The broader embedding starts with the rollout of the business case (which should be considered as a business or project plan) and all of its aspects;

Once these aspects have been put to work and have been tested, the selection and enrollment of students can be initiated, followed by a process of end-user coaching;

Special attention should also go to processes surrounding the re-integration of new knowledge from the collaborative learning space and knowledge tank.

Appendix

Current Research into ICT Supported Learner-Centered Learning Approaches

1. INTRODUCTION

This chapter positions the research reported on in this book in a broader academic perspective. It provides further supporting evidence from a more academic point of view. We will discuss experiences in the use of virtual learning environments for the delivery of management education and the available evidence for a learner-centered model. Our research also considers the fundamental question as to whether the approach chosen in this book represents a viable way of delivering management education.

Research on the practice and practicability of learner-centered learning approaches for continuous learning takes place around three axes, that have to do with the traditional educational model that has been in use now for almost ten centuries. Traditional learning as it takes place in schools and universities, as well as in corporate settings, uses a classroom, teacher centered, and knowledge transfer based approach. The current use of ICT in virtual education often only reemphasizes this approach.

The key research questions in this field are related to the following topics:
- What is the experience with ICT for management education?
- Does a constructivist paradigm support learning better?
- Is there evidence that a learner-centered approach improves learning?

Learner-centered approaches differ from traditional teacher-centered instruction models in a number of ways. Instead of following a learning process driven by the instructor's agenda, students engage in activities that develop their knowledge, and a process enhanced through co-participation with members of a shared learning community. Individuals are therefore absorbed in a process of making sense, conducted through individual and collective learning activities, anchored within specific contexts. This learning philosophy treats individuals as independent, though networked, learners, able to develop their own knowledge and mental models.

Technological innovation presents us with the opportunity to explore whether this way of learning can be delivered effectively in a virtual environment. Recent developments in the design of web-based tools for communication and problem-solving suggest that new pedagogical models are possible, based on "conversational" rather than "instructional" interaction between faculty and students (Ravitz, 1997). This opens up new ways of delivering courses, based on collaborative and skills-based learning.

Research undertaken by Walker and Baets (2000) exactly seeks to test these assumptions in management education by comparing traditional modes of course delivery with hybrid approaches, which introduce virtual learning to the management curriculum. The research measures the contribution that a virtual learning environment can make to student learning, when combined with classroom instruction. Focus lies on the development of the meta-cognitive ability and reflective thinking as outcomes of student learning, following different modes of course delivery.

Summarizing, the key concerns of this appendix are organized around the following sections:

- Knowledge and learning: what research offers us;
- The constructivist paradigm: can learning be co-created?
- Research into learner-centered instructional models;
- A review of current research on the use of ICT for management education.

2. KNOWLEDGE AND LEARNING: WHAT RESEARCH OFFERS US

Central to the learning approach advocated in this book is the concept of knowledge and the way it influences our views on teaching and learning. We embrace the principle that knowledge cannot be represented objectively. In essence, this means that there are no objective models that can truly represent knowledge independent of the human being. Such an approach challenges the positivist assertion that knowledge can be construed independently of the observer, the "knower." It suggests a new way of perceiving the learning process – based on the experiences and activities of the learner.

Traditionally, management theory has drawn its theoretical and methodological inspiration from the social sciences, and especially economics, psychology and sociology. The social sciences were forged and framed around the preoccupation with securing "objective" representations of human behavior and social institutions (in other words, scientific knowledge) for purposes of controlling (Habermas, 1970) and/or disciplining (Foucault, 1979) aspects of the social world. Believing that there is no ontological discontinuity between physical nature and human beings, mainstream social scientists have subscribed to a methodology that has been referred to as positivist in nature.

Giddens (1974) sums up the positivist tradition according to three main principles:

- The concepts and methods of the natural sciences are the most appropriate for studying human activity;
- Knowledge arises from direct perceptions of the world, and nothing is real which is not knowable in this way;
- Value judgments are not knowable in this way and are inappropriate to scientific enquiry.

These principles have underpinned and legitimized management theory, supporting and sustaining the objectives of practicing managers to control and manipulate both employees and consumers (MacIntyre, 1981). Specifically the more recent innovations such as total quality management (TQM) and business process re-engineering (BPR) have sought to establish objective truths about how the "real world" works (see also Van der Linden and Parker, 1999). "Whether it is 'one best way,' continuous improvement or customer-oriented process change, all of these approaches accord with the postulates of positivism in which knowledge is a product of direct observation, and where there exists a unitary and objective truth to be understood independently of the judgements of the observer. (Grey, Knights and Willmott, 1996)

According to this philosophy, knowledge can be completely and correctly structured in terms of entities, attributes and relations that exist (Van der Linden, 1995). The world is real and structured and this structure can be modeled for the learner. The role of teachers is therefore clear, they must select a body of this knowledge, organize it, and deliver it to students. The goal of learners is to acquire this knowledge. Students are expected to absorb the material as passive recipients, and then feed it back in essays and exams. In order to be successful, students must therefore internalize and become technically proficient with what is served.

Management knowledge is as such represented as a "fixed" entity – a "property" that can be traded like a commodity in exchange for other goods. We may refer to this as preceptual knowledge: knowledge of precepts, of givens, of what is "definitely known" in a subject (Laurillard, 1987). This perspective lends itself very much to a teacher-centered paradigm of instruction – a didactic model of educational delivery.

The policy, systems and evaluations in our education systems today focus on the outcomes of a "learning" that has been structured systematically to form an edifice of required knowledge. "Good teaching" is rooted in scientifically valid theories, and logical, technically rational procedures for the relating of these concepts to wider contexts, for the presentation of material to students, and for the assessment of the learning outcomes. In seeking to achieve understanding on the part of students, we usually seek a reformulation or replication of our own understanding. Hence, teaching success is seen as obtaining the "right answers" from students via rational, logical processes only, and teaching and learning are assessed by the end results, usually a quantifiable mark for an examination or course paper. Appraisal of teaching quality and of student learning relies on measurable outputs, linear structure, and on cause and effect relationships (Aram and Noble, 1999).

This interpretation of management pedagogy, founded on positivist thinking and a body of preceptual knowledge, is one that we choose to reject in this book. We want to do so for the following reasons.

First, one important assumption, linked to this philosophy of teaching and learning, is that knowledge can be delivered, acquired and tested objectively. This statement deserves careful consideration. In essence, it suggests that teaching and testing procedures can be grounded within an objectivist paradigm. But to what extent is this really possible? The way one professor teaches is different from the way another teaches so, the content is in fact subject-dependent. We call it "subject matter," even though we consider it to be an objective quantity of transferable knowledge.

Second, we have the assumption that management knowledge can be construed independently of the observer, the "knower." Simply by absorbing the truths transmitted by the instructor, a student can acquire a mastery of the discipline, irrespective of his background, interests, social environment etc. There is no acknowledgement here of the significance of a student's previous knowledge and work experience in the learning and knowledge-building process. Neither is there any consideration of the process by which a student transfers class-based learning to the workplace. This pedagogical theory assumes that a mastery of the truths delivered by the instructor will lead to effective work-based practice. As Raelin (2000) observes, this is rarely the case. Traditional, management education has failed to separate class-based learning from the workplace, resulting in poor levels of transfer in managerial tasks. Learners struggle to incorporate class based lessons into their jobs, when they are subject to conventional classroom instruction.

Third, another premise that we should address is the underlying belief in (absolute) causality and (environmental) determinism in mainstream management theory (Van der Linden and Parker, 1999). The managerial world is determined by clear-cut connections between cause and effect in the sense that managerial actions lead to predictable outcomes and thus to control. The underlying assumption here is that by learning the universal and objective truths of management theory, students will be able to control their own work environments.

All of these assumptions seem to clash with the way in which the world really works: a chaotic and dynamic environment that does not conform to rational and objective techniques of management (Van der Linden, 1996). There exists no scope in traditional objectivist pedagogy for the unpredictable and paradoxical. As Grey and Mitev (1995) remark, there lies an inherent threat to students in terms of the relevance of the knowledge they acquire following this educational process.

Mastering rational and objective techniques preserves the illusion that technical fixes are neutral and universally applicable, and contributes to the building of specialized knowledge which others do not possess, hence justifying management roles and strengthening managerial control. This approach supports a restricted understanding of the world, which is justified through a commitment to commonsense (Grey and Mitev, 1995).

What is required instead is a new model of teaching and learning, which values student experiences and acknowledges the complexity of the "real world." The emphasis should be placed on the learner, not the teacher, with students engaging in active learning in order to acquire the skills to survive in an ever-changing world. Raelin (2000) sums up this critique of conventional pedagogy, arguing for a learner-centered model to replace current methodologies, reflective practice, and real-world activities.

3. THE CONSTRUCTIVIST PARADIGM: CAN LEARNING BE CO-CREATED?

The developments advocated in this book are clearly based on a critique of the objectivist approach to teaching and learning. In other words, we want to explore an alternative interpretation of knowledge, using constructivist principles. The constructivist approach assumes that individuals impose meaning on the world rather than it existing in the world independently of us.

Because any number of different meanings and interpretations can be imposed on the world, there is no such thing as a correct meaning that can be found. Reliable knowledge about the world does not necessarily exist. Instead, our knowledge of the world is construed by ourselves based on prior experience of, and in interaction with, the world. Every person constructs a different perception of the same world. This subjective bias is mediated through the social negotiation of meaning that lends itself to producing a superficial objective reality. It is important, however, to remember that this "objective" reality is actually socially negotiated and constructed (Duffy and Jonassen, 1992).

The constructivist paradigm provides a new way of looking at the learning process. Knowledge is no longer viewed as a fixed commodity, which can be measured and known objectively. It is not independent of the learner, but is internally construed by the learner as a way of making meaning of experiences. This paradigm argues that individuals make meaning out of their own experiences and thus the knowledge constructed by each learner is unique (Barrows and Tamblyn, 1980; Van der Linden, 1996).

Barrows and Tamblyn (1980) define the key principles of constructivist theory about learning as follows :
- Learning involves active construction of a personal, conceptual knowledge base by the learner;
- Learning is reflective as it builds on, and also develops the learner's existing knowledge;
- Learning benefits from multiple views of a subject area;
- Learning is facilitated by authentic activity relevant to the situation in which it is applied.

These principles are implemented in a number of learning models of which the experiential cycle originated by Kolb (1983) is probably the best known. There are many versions of this cycle, but they all emphasize reflective conceptualization and practical experience. This cycle is introduced in chapter 2, as the basis for our proposed virtual approach.

Reflection – is associated with the formation of concepts and is implicit in the formation of concept maps and schemas. Both of these structures reinforce the idea that knowledge is composed of relatively discrete, linked conceptual objects;
Practice – relates to experiential learning and experimentation stages in the learning cycle as well as the authentic activity of constructivist theory. It is associated with the development of subject specific skills and with the learning process itself.

Constructivist theory therefore depicts cognition as an active process, based on action and interpretation. Individuals become builders of facts in constructing contents of knowledge, rather than passive recipients of knowledge from the instructor. Learning consists of constructing knowledge in a way that is authentic, situated, and multi-perspective. Consequently, learners should be engaged in active, constructive, intentional, authentic, and cooperative learning (Jonassen et al, 1995).

This theory offers a fresh perspective for management education, suggesting that learning is an active process involving the construction of knowledge rather than the mastery of one unitary body of truths. The theory acknowledges that there are different forms of knowledge, including tacit or personal knowledge and experiential knowledge (Kolb, 1983). It supports a process of knowing by which individuals engage with their own reality.

Through dialogue with others and themselves they give meaning to the world.

The constructivist theory therefore challenges many of the philosophical assumptions about teaching and learning embedded in traditional management education. One of the fundamental instructional goals of the traditional approach is accurate transmission and reception of knowledge. Communication between the instructor and learner, in this view, is simply a means to an end – a strategy to support the acquisition of knowledge. From the constructivist perspective, instruction should be viewed in a different light: it is not the process of carefully arranged prescriptive strategies, but of coming to understand how people make meaning, and then to create learning environments that promote this construction.

In this perspective, outcomes refer to the knowledge, competencies and skills developed by individual learners. Each of these outcomes represents practical accomplishments by the learner, developed in collaboration with other people. Gheradi, Nicolini and Odella (1998) concur with this view, suggesting that we view knowledge as a participatory activity. The authors suggest that knowledge is not what resides in a person's head or in books or in data banks. Rather, to know is to be capable of participating with the requisite competence in the complex web of relationships among people and activities. Hence, learning is always a practical accomplishment. This view, consistent with our approach, suggests that knowledge is not a stable or static body of facts, but rather a process of making sense by individuals in collaboration with others. Cognition is enacted and can exist only in action and interpretation. Learning becomes a process of acquiring knowledge-in-action.

This interpretation of knowledge also challenges us to find new ways of measuring learning outcomes. Traditional instructional models see learning as the end result of a process of transmitting and transferring knowledge. According to this model teaching is successful when learners will "have" what the teacher transmitted; when it is unsuccessful, they will not (Brown and Duguid, 1992). Traditionally, it is assumed knowledge can be measured easily by assessing whether learners have absorbed the instructor's teaching. This is done through examinations and tests that focus on the ability of students to recall and reconstruct target knowledge, independent of context and learner.

From a constructivist perspective however, this is not an acceptable way of measuring learning. Knowledge is not the product of a passive learning process. It cannot be measured simply by testing students on their ability to replicate and structure information according to the instructor's mental models. Instead, it is embodied in the actions and situations in which it is created. Jonassen (1992) argues for a new system of measurement involving the assessment of learning and student performance within realistic settings, such as the workplace, where students interact with colleagues and peers. In such a setting, students are required to build knowledge and acquire expertise, while performing authentic tasks. In this process, knowledge and meaning are more subjectively determined, grounded in perception and grown out of experience, compared to the more objectivist approaches of assessment. They are more oriented towards measurements of output results. Constructivist evaluation, on the other hand, concentrates on the process of acquiring expertise. It is a continuous process.

In the purest sense, constructivist evaluation should be goal free. Merrill (1992) notes that constructivist theorists view the role of the student to be that of a judge, deciding on the appropriate means of assessment on the most appropriate components of a task. It is self-organized and self-adaptive. This is a difficult position to sustain for university education and its purposes. Taking into account the need for uniform and consistent measurement of learning outcomes for all students so that a degree-granting procedure can be validated, we need to look for an alternative method. A possible way is to view the evaluation as a process of mutually agreed goals between students and the course instructor, allowing the instructor to support individuals in the performance of the learning tasks. Students are allowed to devise their own tasks, and observe their own knowledge construction in association with the degree-granting body. In keeping with the constructivist perspective, evaluation will not be centered on the "reinforcement of behavior," but will serve as a "mirror for viewing the construction process" (Jonassen, 1992).

In other words, we could relate learning outcomes to the tasks that students have agreed to perform within the setting of their own company. Learning will be measured by the extent to which students can transfer conceptual knowledge to practical tasks (and back). Skills and competencies will be viewed as the components that support students in the performance of these tasks. In particular, we refer here to the skills and activities that help managers to learn effectively within the "knowledge society." Pedler, Burgoyne and Boydell already referred in 1978 to these as "meta-qualities" – allowing managers to develop situation-specific skills that they may need. Raelin (2000) provides a different description, referring to them as "meta-competencies." In essence, they describe the communication skills that support collaborative learning, experience-sharing and reciprocal teaching between peers. In addition to these, we refer also to the meta-cognitive knowledge and skills that help managers to solve problems, handle information and transfer their learning to new and unfamiliar contexts and problems. In this respect, Van der Linden (1995, 1996) suggests that managers no longer hold a unique role or position in organizations; they are themselves subject and object in turbulent networks. In this, management has a clear rhetorical function: it has to produce new language games - meaningful contexts or enabling constraints - with their own particular grammar.

Meta-cognitive skills are those that support this process of building knowledge. Reflection-in-action and reflection on experience are central to this process. Meta-cognitive skills should therefore be measured against the ability of learners to engage in reflective conversations with situations – drawing on experience to understand events, attempt to frame problems, suggest actions and reinterpret situations in the light of consequences of action (Raelin, 2000).

4. RESEARCH INTO LEARNER-CENTERED INSTRUCTIONAL MODELS

The learner-centered approach to instruction and course design is based exclusively on constructivist principles. Students are expected to engage in activities that build their own knowledge. This approach reflects a paradigm in which learners seek to explore their own "truths" or "understanding." In this light, we are obliged to redefine what we mean by management knowledge.

Management knowledge no longer relates to the accumulation of knowledge from textbooks, but exists instead in terms of individual learners seeking to evolve their own knowledge and mental models. The learner is an active participant, reflecting on his or her own learning pathway. For university education, this demands an evolution in the roles of both teacher and student, a departure from traditional pedagogical models. It also requires a shift in language in order to redefine the learning process.

Knowles (1985) suggests that we should change the way we refer to instruction, dropping the term "pedagogy" which becomes redundant when we refer to learner-centered instructional strategies for adults. He observes that the learner-centered model of instruction is suited more to andragogy (a model based around adult educational requirements), rather than pedagogy. Following Knowles' thinking, we can identify five important differences between pedagogical (teacher-centered) and learner-centered strategies in terms of our perception of the learner (based on Knowles, 1985):

Self-directed rather than submissive: pedagogically the learner is regarded as a dependent person, with the teacher held responsible for the "what, when and how" of learning, as well as any assessment of whether the learning has occurred. The submissive learner can be contrasted with the andragogical model of the self-directed learner. In order for the self-directed learner to flourish, a learning environment ought to be characterized by mutual respect, trust, and collaboration between students and instructor.

Experience valued as a learning resource: the dominant learning mode in traditional pedagogy is transmission from teacher to student. Adults, however, have a great volume and variety of experience, which should be valued and viewed as an important learning resource. This is particularly the case in management, when many of the learning objectives relate to work-based experiences.

Readiness to learn: following the traditional pedagogical model, students are taught when they are deemed ready to learn. Andragogically, learners determine what and when they wish to learn – when they perceive a need to know (just in time). In terms of management learning, this may be when they decide that some part of their job performance requires improvement.

Orientation to learning: traditional curricular arrangements are subject-oriented – learners follow a preset curriculum. The andragogical model situated the curricular content around the needs and interests of the learner. For adults, requirements tend to be more problem or task-centered. Adults make a conscious decision to learn because of a particular need, and the more clearly the "need to know" can be determined and the processes of learning made relevant to the satisfaction of that need, the more likely is the learning to be effective.

Self-motivation: According to the andragogical model, learners are self-motivated – motivated through the wish to do a job more effectively and achieve greater recognition for it, alongside the capacity to have more influence in the work situation.

Based on this classification, the learner is transformed from a passive to an active participant in the educational process. Students are viewed holistically as people with intelligence, experience and social capabilities. Learning is influenced by the learners' cognitive and emotional interpretation of situations as they interact with their environment in their attempts to achieve their learning goals. The instructor's role changes too, shifting from a teaching role to one of facilitation. Chung (1991) notes that within a constructivist learning environment the relationship between teacher and student is characterized by shared knowledge among teachers and students, shared authority and responsibility, with the teacher adapting to the role of guide in the instructional process. In this new collaborative relationship, the instructor helps students to diagnose their own learning needs, supports learners in formulating their learning objectives, encouraging them to discover knowledge and build their own mental models. The instructor also helps students to evaluate their own learning.

Hence, learning should be viewed as a dynamic process. It flows from the interaction of each individual within the learning content, activities and environment. It is therefore based on social interaction. Learning is no longer conceived as just an individual phenomenon, but as one that involves the whole community. Constructivists view learning as a social dialogical process in which communities of practitioners socially negotiate the meaning of phenomena (Jonassen et al., 1995). This idea suggests that important characteristics of learning involve collaboration among communities of individuals, language as the medium of the message, and conversation as the process by which meaning is constructed (Miller and Miller, 1999).

Consequently, the learner-centered approach requires a collaborative dimension to be included within the instructional process. A dominant characteristic of constructivist learning is collaboration among learners. In contrast to objectivist instructional theories, constructivist theories claim that it is through communication with others that learners construct meaning from their experiences. As a result, it is the importance of social negotiation in the learning processes that makes communication critical (Miller and Miller, 1999).

It is clear that the collaborative dimension serves as a useful point of distinction between learner-centered and teacher-centered instructional strategies. The predominant communication configuration in learner-centered course design is that of learners to learners (i.e., many-to-many). This is quite different from the traditional approach to course delivery, which can be described as a lecture-based approach to learning (one-to-many). In the traditional model, the instructor controls the learning – determining what is learned and how the learning is conducted – usually through a combination of lectures and preparatory work to be completed by the student. For this approach, the communication configuration is based around the instructor and groups of students, with the emphasis placed on the transmission of knowledge.

The choice of instructional strategy will therefore strongly influence the level of interaction between students as well as the degree of control exercised by them in the learning process. It should also have a direct influence over the design of the learning environment, the place of 'interaction.'

5.   A REVIEW OF CURRENT RESEARCH ON THE USE OF ICT FOR MANAGEMENT EDUCATION

In this section we will investigate the relationship between computer technologies and instructional strategies. We will consult the existing research within the field of management education, in addition to the general educational technology research that is available. Our discussion will focus on the way in which computers have been used to deliver education to students till now. We will also consider the instructional models that have been employed, and the learning outcomes that have been reported for computer-mediated course delivery.

The introduction of information technology as a way of delivering management education is a recently established phenomenon. It is most commonly associated with open universities, with the aim to support distance-learning programs. However, regular universities have also made great progress in using ICT – particularly "knowledge media" – to support conversational paradigms and community ideas in management education.

An integral part of this new trend in course delivery has been the use of different kinds of computer mediated communication systems (or CMC). This technology has been selected to support ongoing discussion between instructors and students – allowing each to express their viewpoints. It has been used either as a supplement to classroom teaching (an added extra, to support social contact and interaction out-of-class), or as a central part of the delivery and assessment framework for courses. Research findings regarding the added value of using this technology for teaching and learning have been quiet mixed. Within the field of management education, there have only been a limited number of studies conducted, which have produced inconclusive results.

First, we will summarize the main findings emerging from studies on electronic learning, in order to provide a broad insight into the value of this technology for (university) education.

5.1.   What is understood by Computer Mediated Communicaton?

Let us begin with a definition of Computer Mediated Communication or CMC. CMC systems include all forms of communication that occur over a network of computers. It is described as being able to "support interaction between students and tutors over long distances. For those purposes, CMC may include electronic mail, computer conferencing, computer bulletin boards, facsimile, teletex and videotex, voice messaging and desktop videoconferencing." (Akehurst, 1996)

Communications via CMC systems usually occur asynchronously, although occasionally users do coordinate times when they are "online" together. The asynchronous nature of these systems is often cited as a positive benefit to busy workers and learners who prefer the flexibility of communicating whenever it suits them. The nature of electronic meetings – the social presence, process and outcomes – differ from face to face meetings and possibly require new ways of thinking about the meaning of group work when it is mediated via computers (McConnell, 1990).

The structural features of a conferencing system include e-mail messaging, asynchronous and synchronous conferencing tools for group discussion, and a bulletin board for posting news and discussion items. Members of a computer conference are therefore able to carry out a number of basic operations such as:
-   Reading the text of a conference
-   Adding their own items (freestanding textual communications to the conference)
-   Adding responses to other people's conference items (or even to their own items)
-   Sending private messages to any number of individual conference members.

The technology allows participants to communicate on a one-to-one or one-to-group basis via the conference system. CMC is used most commonly as a way of supporting group discussion between participants on an asynchronous basis. This is similar to participation in a normal conference discussion, but via text alone and over a much longer span of time.

Laurillard (1993) notes that from a pedagogical perspective, computer conferencing is believed to possess a number of advantages over normal face-to-face discussions. Students can take time to ponder the various points made in a discussion group, and can make their contribution in their own time. Topic negotiation is also possible as in face-to-face discussion. An instructor may pursue several lines of discussion with different students within one conference, though a good moderator would probably separate them out into different 'topics' within the conference. This type of technology is ideally suited to the work of distance learning universities, connecting students who are unable to meet on a face-to-face basis. As such, it has become a distinguishing feature of "third-generation" distance education (online education), supporting social rather than individual learning processes. The advantages for campus-based students are less clear however. Laurillard (1993) points out that in both cases the pedagogical benefits of the medium will rest entirely on how successfully it supports a "fruitful dialogue" between tutor and students, or between fellow students.

5.2.   CMC and general educational research

General educational research has accounted for a number of claims being made for conferencing technology, particularly regarding the value it can bring to student learning. We will sum up some of the main contributions in this section.

Computer-mediated communication is used as a tool in maturing students' learning styles and developing independent learning strategies. Within the context of an online course, students can be asked to reflect on what they already know and to share their experience or expertise in certain areas of the course with everyone in the group, by making a presentation or fielding questions. Computer conferencing also makes the valuable technique of cooperative projects available to distance learners, so that a small group of students can work together on a joint paper, presentation, or assignment (Mason and Kaye, 1990).

Brandt and Briggs (1995) pointed out in a study on electronic meeting systems in a university classroom, that participation levels increased significantly between students and provided a "direct support for cooperative learning." Turoff (1991) also observed that conferencing in its asynchronous mode offered potential for real improvement in the group process, promoting high interaction levels among participants and effective cooperative learning. Lave and Wenger (1991) and Rogoff (1990), on the other hand, have suggested that from a learning environment or community standpoint, students have greater opportunities with electronic collaboration tools to solicit and share knowledge, while developing common ground or intersubjectivity with their peers and teachers.

Harasim (1989) gathered evidence that online courses can fit the learner-centered model of learning. Student interactions have involved dynamic and extensive sharing of information, ideas, and opinions among learners. Based on these observations she claims that knowledge building occurs as students explore issues, examine one another's arguments, agree, disagree, and question positions. As a result, collaboration contributes to higher order learning through cognitive restructuring or conflict resolution, in which new ways of understanding the material emerge as a result of contact with new or different perspectives.

There are a number of studies that support these conclusions on cognition and knowledge construction. It was noted that networked collaborative classrooms enable students to go increasingly deeper into their own understanding of the subject, enabling them to glimpse questions and contradictions that demand their attention. Turoff (2000) has argued that the combination of conferencing technology with face-to-face classes stresses a number of cognitive benefits for students, including enriched and deeper learning through ongoing course discussion and collaborative problem solving. Hara, Bonk and Angeli (2000) confirm this observation in their own content analysis of electronic learning activity for a graduate level educational psychology course. They conclude that by using CMC, students have more time to reflect on course content and make in-depth cognitive and social contributions to a college class than would be possible in a traditional classroom setting.

A cautionary note should be recorded here though, since most research is based on only a limited amount of evidence. Moreover, the research that has been conducted clearly lacks a longitudinal perspective.

In the absence of these types of studies, it is hard to judge the true value of conferencing on the learning process. One of the major limitations regarding the research to date on CMC is that it does not measure the impact of conferencing tools on student course performance, nor does it consider the long term retention of course material. As a result, many of the claims made regarding conferencing technologies and the support it offers for "higher order learning" are assumed rather than proven. As Laurillard (1993) notes, learning through discussion remains one of the great untested assumptions of current educational practice. The quality of the learning that takes place and the value of student interactions have not been thoroughly investigated.

The degree to which CMC supports a "learner-centered" curriculum is also open to question. Hara, Bonk and Angeli (2000) observed that computer mediated learning has been commonly used by instructors as a supplement to the teacher-centered curriculum, rather than as a means of offering a new method of pedagogical delivery. From this perspective, we must question the extent to which students are free to take charge of their own learning. As studies by Hara et al. (2000) and Mowrer (1996) have shown, ensuring high quality engagement in online activity is a much harder phenomenon to deliver and research.

Technological features do not ensure effective communication, and technical linkage alone does not create community. While the attributes of the networks enable significant advantages for human communication, they are not a guarantee (Harasim, 1993). These studies suggest that student-centered learning is not a natural consequence of this form of course delivery. Much will depend on the course design and type of activities to be performed, as well as the individual characteristics of learners and instructors - their background and attitudes.

5.3. ICT and management education

Whereas the previous section reported on CMC and education in general, we would like to concentrate in this section on the application of ICT (a bit broader than CMC) particularly in management education.

Over recent years, universities and business schools view ICT as a means by which collaborative learning can be introduced to management courses, either distance or campus based. For example, UK institutions such as Henley and Lancaster have replaced part of the face-to-face content of their management programs with ICT based activity. The UK Open University too has played a major role in experimenting with ICT applications and their impact on the learning process. An attempt has been made to use this medium as a means to develop "conversational" rather than "instructional" interaction between faculty and students.

In particular, the value of computer mediated learning for "out-of-class" knowledge sharing and discussion has been emphasized in a number of research studies such as Hardy, Hodgson, McConnell and Reynolds (1991), Akehurst (1996), and Hartley et al. (1994).

Research suggests that ICT has been used to support a teacher-centered curriculum – an observation consistent with the findings of general educational researchers such as Hara, Bonk and Angeli (2000). While it is true that computer technologies have been used to support conversational paradigms and community ideas in management education, the overall pedagogical paradigm has not changed. Students are encouraged to use the technology to discuss issues of the course predetermined by the instructor, to engage within a teacher-centered curriculum. Instructors are still central to the learning process, challenging students to engage in collaborative activities according to their own frame of reference (Leidner and Jarvenpaa, 1995).

According to Leidner and Jarvenpaa, the impact of these initiatives has been to automate and facilitate information flows between an instructor and students or among students. In many instances, computers and communication technologies have replaced or augmented blackboards and chalk for instructors and paper and pencils for students. The danger exists here for instructors simply to use the technology to replicate traditional models of teaching.

Bearing the necessary reservations in mind, research supports the approach described in this book. But it must be clear that what we are witnessing with these developments in course design and delivery are changes that amount to little more than "technological evolution," rather than a fundamental paradigm shift in the way that students are educated. Hence, the implementation of a learner-centered approach to education is still in its infancy.

5.4.   Some more recent trends

The work of Leidner and Jarvenpaa (1995) is insightful in this respect, helping us to rethink our approach to education technology and its relevance for teaching purposes. They define the relationship between technology and learning according to two process dimensions:

- Control of the pace and content of learning
- The purpose of instruction (knowledge dissemination and knowledge creation)

They argue that learner-centered education can only be delivered with technologies that place much of the control of the content and pace of learning in the hands of students, not the instructor. The purpose of using instructional technology should move away from knowledge dissemination toward knowledge creation. The instructor should no longer be the primary creator of the knowledge. Instead, students become a very important part of the knowledge creation process, with the instructor serving as a mediator rather than a dictator of the learning process.

According to their vision, technologies that deliver control of the pace and rhythm of learning to students are the only appropriate tools to support constructive and collaborative learning. They hold the key to conceptual learning and higher-order thinking, facilitating student access to information to improve the availability or reality of learning materials. In their opinion, virtual learning spaces represent an appropriate form of technology that can support learner-centered outcomes. In this way, the technology enables students to construct new knowledge from existing sources.

Models that are more elaborate include virtual environments, where hypertext is used to link information in the form of an integrated knowledge platform. Virtual environments also include a communication platform, so that individuals are able to interact with each other, as well with the information contained within the platform. In such cases, it is the quality and density of the communication that the virtual platform supports, that enables a new paradigm of instruction to be delivered. Another question relates to the dynamic properties of the learning process within this medium, supporting experience-sharing, sense-making and knowledge instruction between individuals (Britain and Liber, 1999). Leidner and Jarvenpaa (1995) concluded that the virtual learning space support cognitive, constructivist, collaborative, and socio-cultural learning outcomes.

Some other studies on collaborative learning in a virtual learning space have supported the fact that for mature, motivated learners this mode of learning can be more effective than the traditional classroom (Hiltz, 1988; Singer, et al., 1988; Walker and Baets, 2000). Studies including less motivated and less mature learners observed the opposite effect. Students lacking the necessary basic skills and self-discipline may do better in a traditionally delivered mode (Hiltz, 1988).

As Leidner and Jarvenpaa (1995) point out, students are as responsible in the virtual learning space for the quality and amount of learning as the instructor. Students accustomed to traditional teaching methods may be unwilling and/or unable to adjust to the additional responsibility placed on them.

6.   CONCLUDING REMARKS

Having established the reasoning for a constructivist (learner-centered) pedagogy for management education earlier, we should now consider the contribution computer-mediated learning can make to this form of learning. In essence, can a case be made for the use of computer technologies in the design and delivery of management education?   To what extent can computer technologies support constructivist outcomes for management education?

The way course materials are organized and presented to students within the learning environment, is important according to constructive theorists. Thompson (1999) states that the instructor's role - following the cognitive constructivist paradigm – is to arrange instructional conditions that foster students' construction of knowledge.   The arrangement of the course material should allow a degree of learner control as to what information will be accessed and in what order. Paquette (1998) argues that this can best be achieved by making information available to the learner at the moment it is required, as well as by providing individualized learning pathways for pro-active knowledge-building within the learning environment.

Researchers such as Paquette argue that virtual learning environments (or VLEs) can provide a suitable platform for the delivery of courses, which are designed according to constructivist principles. VLEs represent learning management software systems that synthesize the functionality of computer-mediated communications software (e-mail, bulletin boards, newsgroups etc.) and online methods of delivering course materials (the World Wide Web). They can be designed to accommodate a wide range of learning styles and goals, to encourage collaborative and resource-based learning, and to allow sharing and reuse of resources (Britain and Liber, 1999).

VLEs offer an integrated knowledge platform, linking information and activities through hypertext links. They can also provide synchronous and asynchronous communication tools to support communication among learners (many-to-many). Paquette (1998) notes that virtual environments can include five major spaces for user interaction:

- An *information space* - containing documents and data to support the knowledge-building process;
- A *production space* - in which tools are provided to help students in the development of assignments;

- A *collaboration space* - providing the necessary tools to exchange files with other participants, and to support synchronous and asynchronous communication;
- An *assistance space* - where help and advice are available from a resource person or the computerized system;
- A *self-management space* - for organization of activities within the environment and navigation.

The integration of these functions within one learning system distinguishes virtual environments from computer-mediated communication and conferencing tools. According to Paquette, they help to position the learner at the center of the learning system, helping him/her to transform information into knowledge.

We conclude this discussion by stating that theoretical support does indeed exist for a relationship between computer technology and constructivist learning. Technologies are available that can and do support constructivist learning. On the other hand, there is no reported evidence yet, as to how and to what degree virtual environments contribute to the effective learning of individuals. It is far from proven in real life cases, to what extent virtual learning technologies support constructivist learning outcomes - the foundation for the learner-centered approach.

REFERENCES

Akehurst, E. (1996) "The Use of Computer Mediated Communication as a Tool in the Delivery of Distance Learning Based MBA Programmes," Working Paper, Henley Research Centre, Henley Management College, UK.

Aram, E. & Noble, D. (1999) "Educating Prospective Managers in the Complexity of Organizational Life," in "Management Learning," vol. 30 (3) pp. 321-342.

Barrows, H.S. & Tamblyn, R.M. (1980) "Problem-Based Learning: An Approach to Medical Education," New York: Springer Publishing Co.

Brandt, S. & Briggs, R.O. (1995) "Exploring the Use of EMS in the Classroom: Two Field Studies," in R. Sprague, et. al. (Eds.) "Proceedings of the 28th Annual International Conference on System Science."

Britain, S. & Liber, O. (1999) "A Framework for Pedagogical Evaluation of Virtual Learning Environments" - http://www.jtap.ac.uk/reports/htm/jtap-041.html

Brown, J. S. and Duguid, P., (1992) "Stolen Knowledge" in "Educational Technology Publications": http://www.parc.xerox.com/ops/members/brown/papers/stolenknow.html

Chung, J. (1991) "Collaborative learning strategies: The design of instructional environments for the emerging new school," in "Educational Technology," 31(6), 1991, pp.15-22.

Duffy, T. & Jonassen, D.H. (1992) "Constructivism: New Implications for Instructional Technology, in Thomas M. Duffy & David H. Jonassen (Eds.), "Constructivism and the Technology of Instruction: A Conversation," Hillsdale, N.J., London: Erlbaum, 1992.

Foucault, M. (1979) "The Order of Things," Tavistock, London, UK.

Gheradi, S., Nicolini, D., & Odella,F. (1998) "Towards a Social Understanding of How People Learn in Organizations: The Notion of Situated Curriculum" in "Management Learning," vol. 29 (3): 273-297.

Giddens, A. (1974) "Positivism and Sociology," Heinemann, London, UK.

Grey, C., Knights, D., & Willmott, H., (1996) "Is a Critical Pedagogy of Management Possible?" in French, R. and Grey, C. (Eds.) "Rethinking Management Education," Sage Publications, London, pp. 94-110.

Grey, C. & Mitev, N. (1995), "Management Education; A Polemic," in "Management Learning" vol. 26 no. 1, Sage Publications, London, UK.

Habermas, J. (1970) "Knowledge and Human Interests". Heinemann, London, UK.

Hara, N., Bonk, C.J., & Angeli, C. (2000). "Content analysis of on-line discussion in an applied educational psychology course," "Instructional Science," 28(2), pp. 115-152

Harasim, L.M., (1993) "Networlds: Networks as Social Space," in Harasim, L.M. (Ed.) "Global Networks: Computers and International Communication," The MIT Press, Cambridge, Mass., USA, p.28.

Harasim, Linda., (1989) "On-Line Education: A New Domain" in Mason, Robin and Kaye, Anthony (eds) "Mindweave," Pergamon Press, Oxford.

Hardy, G., Hodgson, V., McConnell, D., & Reynolds, M., (1991), "Computer Mediated Communication for Management Training and Development," Centre for the Study of Management Learning, The Management School, Lancaster University, UK.

Hartley J. et al., (1994) "The Comparative Evaluation of Computer Conferencing with Other Methods of Teaching and Learning," Department of Organisational Psychology," Birkbeck College, London University, UK.

Hiltz, S.R. (1988) "Collaborative Learning in a Virtual Classroom: Highlights of Findings," in "Proceedings of the Conference on Computer-Supported Cooperative Work," Portland, OR, September 26-28, 1988.

Jonassen, D., Davidson, M., Collins, M., Campbell, J. & Haag, B. (1995) "Constructivism and computer-mediated communication in distance education," in "The American Journal of Distance Education," 9 (2).

Jonassen (1992) "Evaluating Constructivist Learning" in Thomas M. Duffy & David H. Jonassen, (Eds.), "Constructivism and the Technology of Instruction: A Conversation," Hillsdale, N.J., London: Erlbaum, 1992

Knowles, M.S. (1985) "Andragogy in Action," Jossey-Bass, San Francisco, USA.

Kolb, D. A. (1983), "Experiential Learning: Experience as the Source of Learning and Development," Prentice Hall, Englewood Cliffs, New Jersey, USA.

Laurillard, D. (1993) "Rethinking University Teaching: a framework for the effective use of educational technology," Routledge, London, UK, p.168.

Laurillard, D.M. (1987) "Computers and the emancipation of students: giving control to the learner" in "Instructional Science," 16: 3-18.

Lave J., and Wenger, E. (1991) "Situated Learning: Legitimate Peripheral Participation," New York, Cambridge University Press.

Leidner, D. E. and Jarvenpaa, S.L. (1995), "The Use of Information Technology to Enhance Management School Education: A Theoretical View," MIS Quarterly, 19 (3), p. 275.

McConnell, D (1990) "Case Study: The Educational use of Computer Conferencing," "Education and Training Technology International," 27(2), 190-208.

MacIntyre, A. (1981) "After Virtue," London: Duckworth.

Mason, R. & Kaye, T., (1990) "Toward a New Paradigm for Distance Education," in (ed.) Harasim, L.M., "Online Education: Perspectives on a New Environment," Praeger, New York, USA, pp. 25-26.

Merrill (1992) "Constructivism and Instructional Design" in Thomas M. Duffy & David H. Jonassen, (Eds.), "Constructivism and the Technology of Instruction: A Conversation," Hillsdale, N.J., London: Erlbaum, 1992.

Miller, S.M. & Miller, K.L., (1999) "Using Instructional Theory to Facilitate Communication in Web-based Courses," in "Educational Technology & Society" 2 (3) 1999. http://ifets.ieee.org/periodical/vol_3_99/miller.html

Mowrer, D. (1996) "A content analysis of student/instructor communication via computer conferencing," in "Higher Education," 32 (2), pp. 217-241.

Paquette, G., (1998) "Virtual Learning Centers for XX1st-century Organizations," in Verdejo F. & Davies, G. (Eds.) "The Virtual Campus," Chapman & Hall, UK, p.22.

Pedler, Burgoyne and Boydell (1978), "A Manager's Guide to Self Development," McGraw-Hill, Maidenhead, UK.

Raelin, J. A. (2000) "Work-Based Learning: The New Frontier of Management Development" Prentice Hall, Upper Saddle, New Jersey, USA, p.16.

Ravitz, J. (1997) "An ISD model for building online communities: Furthering the dialogue." "Proceedings of the Annual Conference of the Association for Educational Communications and Technology," Washington, D.C.: AECT, http://copernicus.bbn.com/Ravitz/isd_model.html

Rogoff, B. (1990) "Apprenticeship in Thinking: Cognitive Development in Social Context," New York, Oxford.

Singer, J., Behrend, S., and Roschelle, J. (1988) "Children's Collaborative Use of a Computer Microworld," in "Proceedings of the Conference on Computer-Supported Cooperative Work," Portland, OR, September 26-28, 1988.

Thompson, H., (1999) "The Impact of Technology and Distance Education: A Classical Learning Theory Viewpoint," in "Educational Technology & Society" 2 (3) 1999.

Turoff, M. (2000), "An End to Student Segregation: No More Separation Between Distance Learning and Regular Courses," in "On The Horizon," vol. 8 no.1 Jan 2000 – http://horizon.unc.edu/horizon/online/html/8/1/

Turoff, M. (1991), "Computer-Mediated Communication Requirements for Group Support," "Journal of Organizational Computing," 1 (1).

Van der Linden, G., (1995), "Managing and Understanding Perplexities: A Postmodern View on Organizations and Managerial Competencies," Working Papers Series, Nyenrode University Press.

Van der Linden, G. (1996). "Gérer et Comprendre les Interrogations Perplexes." In: Mallet, J. (Ed.). L'Organisation Apprenante. Aix-en-Provence: Univ. de Provence.

Van der Linden, G., and Parker P., (1999), "On Paradoxes between Human Resources Management, Postmodernism, and HR Information Systems," in Baets W. (Ed), A Collection of Essays on Complexity and Management, World Scientific Press.

Walker R. and Baets W., (2000),"Designing a virtual course environment for management education: a learner-centred approach," Indian Journal of Open Learning (IJOL), September, 2000.

Index

219

Author Index